DANIEL

J. Vernon McGee

THOMAS NELSON
Since 1798

NASHVILLE DALLAS MEXICO CITY RIO DE JANEIRO BEIJING

Published in Nashville, Tennessee, by Thomas Nelson, Inc.

Scripture quotations are from the KING JAMES VERSION of the Bible.

Library of Congress Cataloging-in-Publication Data

McGee, J. Vernon (John Vernon), 1904–1988
   [Thru the Bible with J. Vernon McGee]
   Thru the Bible commentary series / J. Vernon McGee.
     p.   cm.
   Reprint. Originally published: Thru the Bible with J. Vernon
McGee. 1975.
   Includes bibliographical references.
   ISBN 0-7852-1028-8 (TR)
   ISBN 0-7852-1087-3 (NRM)
   1. Bible—Commentaries. I. Title.
BS491.2.M37 1991
220.7′7—dc20   90–41340
ISBN: 978-0-7852-0539-5   CIP

Printed in the United States
26 27 28 29 30 EPAC 13 12 11 10 09

CONTENTS

DANIEL

PREFACE

The radio broadcasts of the Thru the Bible Radio five-year program were transcribed, edited, and published first in single-volume paperbacks to accommodate the radio audience.

There has been a minimal amount of further editing for this publication. Therefore, these messages are not the word-for-word recording of the taped messages which went out over the air. The changes were necessary to accommodate a reading audience rather than a listening audience.

These are popular messages, prepared originally for a radio audience. They should not be considered a commentary on the entire Bible in any sense of that term. These messages are devoid of any attempt to present a theological or technical commentary on the Bible. Behind these messages is a great deal of research and study in order to interpret the Bible from a popular rather than from a scholarly (and too-often boring) viewpoint.

We have definitely and deliberately attempted "to put the cookies on the bottom shelf so that the kiddies could get them."

The fact that these messages have been translated into many languages for radio broadcasting and have been received with enthusiasm reveals the need for a simple teaching of the whole Bible for the masses of the world.

I am indebted to many people and to many sources for bringing this volume into existence. I should express my especial thanks to my secretary, Gertrude Cutler, who supervised the editorial work; to Dr. Elliott R. Cole, my associate, who handled all the detailed work with the publishers; and finally, to my wife Ruth for tenaciously encouraging me from the beginning to put my notes and messages into printed form.

Solomon wrote, ". . . of making many books there is no end; and much study is a weariness of the flesh" (Eccl. 12:12). On a sea of books that flood the marketplace, we launch this series of THRU THE BIBLE with the hope that it might draw many to the one Book, *The Bible*.

J. Vernon McGee

The Book of
DANIEL

INTRODUCTION

The Book of Daniel is one of the most thrilling books in the Bible, and it is, of course, a book on prophecy. Because prophecy bulks large in the Bible, I would like to say a word about it before we look at the Book of Daniel specifically. One fourth of the books in the Bible are of prophetic nature; the subject and statement of the books are eschato- logical, that is, they deal with prophecy. One fifth of the content of Scripture was predictive at the time of its writing; a large segment of that has been fulfilled. Therefore, the prophecy in Scripture can be divided into fulfilled and unfulfilled prophecy. We will find a great deal of fulfilled prophecy in Daniel.

There are certain great subjects of prophecy. They are like planes flying into an airport from all sections of the world, and you can go to the Book of Revelation and see all these great subjects brought to a final fruition. The main subject of prophecy is the Lord Jesus Christ. Other topics include Israel, the gentile nations, evil, Satan, the Man of Sin, the Great Tribulation period, and how this age will end. The church is also a subject of prophecy; however, the church is never mentioned in the Old Testament, and therefore there will be no refer- ence to it in the Book of Daniel. Then, of course, there are the subjects of the Kingdom, the Millennium, and eternity future. These are the great subjects of prophecy.

I do not believe that one can have a full-orbed view of the Bible or be a well-rounded student of Scripture without a knowledge of escha- tology, or prophecy. The neglect of the study of prophecy has produced certain harmful results which I think are quite evident today. Many of the cults have gone off the track in prophetic areas. This is largely because the teaching of prophecy has been neglected by the great denominations. For example, Dr. Charles Hodge, a great theologian at Princeton in the past, made this statement: "The subject [prophecy] cannot be adequately discussed without taking a survey of all the prophetic teachings of Scripture both of the Old Testament and of the New. This task cannot be satisfactorily accomplished by anyone who has not made a study of the prophecies a specialty. The author [that is, Dr. Hodge], knowing that he has not such qualifications for the work, purposes to confine himself in a great measure to a historical survey of the different schemes of interpreting the Scriptures prophetically." That certainly was a startling and sad admission on the part of Dr. Hodge. As a result, we find men in a great many of our denominations today who are ill-equipped to speak on prophecy. They dismiss it with a wave of the hand as being unimportant. And those who do go into the study of prophecy often come up with that which is sensational and fanatical. The Book of Daniel, particularly, is the subject of many such sensational writers on prophecy.

The Book of Daniel is a very important one, and it has therefore been the object of special attack by Satan in the same way that the Book of Isaiah has been. Isaiah has been called the prince of the prophets, and I would like to say that Daniel, then, is the king of the prophets. Both of these prophecies are very important in Scripture and have been especially attacked by unbelievers.

The Book of Daniel has been a battlefield between conservative and liberal scholars for years, and much of the controversy has had to do with the dating of the writing of the book. Porphyry, a heretic in the third century A.D. declared that the Book of Daniel was a forgery written during the time of Antiochus Epiphanes and the Maccabees. That would place its writing around 170 B.C., almost four hundred years *after* Daniel lived. The German critics seized upon this hypothesis and, along with Dr. S. R. Driver, developed this type of criticism of the book. These critics, as well as present-day unbelievers, assume the premise that the supernatural does not exist. Since foreknowledge is supernatural, there can, therefore, be no foretelling, no prophesying.

However, the very interesting thing is that the Septuagint, the Greek version of the Old Testament, was translated before the time of Antiochus Epiphanes, and it contains the Book of Daniel! The liberal scholars have ignored similar very clear testimony from the Dead Sea Scrolls. Those scrolls confirm the fact that there was only one author of the Book of Isaiah. The liberal has wanted to argue that there was a duet or even a trio of "Isaiahs" who wrote that book. The Dead Sea Scrolls are very much alive, and they refute the liberal critic on that point.

It is interesting how these questions which are raised concerning the Bible are always answered in time. The heretic, the critic, and the cultist always move in an area of the Bible where we do not have full knowledge at the time. Everyone can speculate, and you can speculate any way you want to—generally the speculation goes the wrong way. However, in time, the Word of God is proven accurate.

Flavius Josephus (*Antiquities of the Jews*, Vol. 1, p. 388) also records an incident during the time of Alexander the Great which supports the early authorship of Daniel. When Alexander's invasion reached the Near East, Jaddua, the high priest, went out to meet him and showed him a copy of the Book of Daniel in which Alexander was clearly mentioned. Alexander was so impressed by this that, instead of destroying Jerusalem, he entered the city peaceably and worshiped at the temple.

These arguments clearly contradict the liberal critics; yet there are those who blindly ignore them. It is not in the purview of these brief comments to enter into useless argument and fight about that which has already been settled. I simply want to say that I accept the findings of conservative scholarship that the man Daniel was not a deceiver and that his book was not a forgery. I feel the statement of Pusey is apropos here: "The rest which has been said is mostly mere insolent assumptions against Scripture, grounded on unbelief." Sir Isaac Newton declared, "To reject Daniel is to reject the Christian religion."

Furthermore, our Lord Jesus called the Pharisees "hypocrites," but He called Daniel "the prophet" (see Matt. 24:15; Mark 13:14). Very frankly, I go along with the Lord Jesus who, by the way, never reversed His statement. The endorsement of the Lord Jesus Christ is valid and sufficient for every believer, whether or not he has examined the arguments of the critics, and it satisfies the sincere saint without his having to study the answers of conservative scholarship.

We know more about Daniel the man than we do of any other prophet. He gives us a personal account of his life from the time he was carried captive to Babylon in the third year of the reign of Jehoiakim (about 606 B.C.) until the first year of King Cyrus (about 536 B.C.). Daniel's life and ministry bridge the entire seventy years of captivity. At the beginning of the book he is a boy in his teens. At the end he is an old man of fourscore and more years.

Here is God's estimate of the man Daniel: "O Daniel, a man greatly beloved" (Dan. 10:11). I would not want to be one of those critics who have called the Book of Daniel a forgery. Someday I am going to face Daniel in heaven and find that he has a pretty good reputation—"a man greatly beloved."

There are three words which characterize Daniel's life: purpose, prayer, and prophecy.

1. Daniel was a man of purpose (Dan. 1:8; 6:10). When the king made a decree that everyone had to eat the same thing, Daniel and his friends decided they would abide by the law of Moses—and they did. Daniel was a man of purpose, and we can see this all the way through his book. Here was a man who stood on his own two feet and had the intestinal fortitude to speak God's Word.

God have pity today on men who claim to be His messengers to the world but haven't got the courage to declare the Word of God. I also thank God that there are many who are declaring the whole Word of God, including prophecy, in our day. You see, the proper study of prophecy will not lead us to sensationalism and fanaticism, but it will lead us to a life of holiness and fear of God. John said in 1 John 3:3, "And every man that hath this hope in him purifieth himself, even as he is pure." The study of prophecy will purify our lives, my friend.

2. Daniel was a man of prayer (Dan. 2:17–23; 6:10; 9:3–19; 10). There are several incidents recorded in this book about Daniel's prayer life. By the way, prayer got Daniel into the lion's den. How about that for answered prayer? Well, God also miraculously saved him from the lions. Daniel was a man of prayer.

3. Daniel was a man of prophecy. The Book of Daniel divides itself equally: the first half is history, and the last half is prophecy. Daniel gives us the skeleton of prophecy on which all prophecy is placed. The image in Nebuchadnezzar's dream (Dan. 2) and the beasts (Dan. 7) are the backbone of prophecy; the Seventy Weeks (Dan. 9) are the ribs which fit into their proper place.

The key verse to the Book of Daniel is Daniel 2:44: "And in the days of these kings shall the God of heaven set up a kingdom, which shall never be destroyed: and the kingdom shall not be left to other people, but it shall break in pieces and consume all these kingdoms, and it shall stand for ever."

Dr. G. Campbell Morgan gave this theme for the Book of Daniel: "Persistent Government of God in the Government of the World." This is the book of the universal sovereignty of God. Prophecy is here interwoven with history to show that God is overruling the idolatry, blasphemy, self-will, and intolerance of the Gentiles.

More especially, Daniel 12:4 brings together ". . . the times of the Gentiles . . ." (Luke 21:24) and "the time of the end" (see also Dan. 8:17; 11:35, 40) for the nation Israel in the Great Tribulation period. This coming crisis eventuates in Christ's setting up the millennial Kingdom. "But thou, O Daniel, shut up the words, and seal the book, even to the time of the end: many shall run to and fro, and knowledge shall be increased" (Dan. 12:4).

The Book of Daniel deals with political issues apart from ecclesiastical matters, giving the final outcome of events and issues which are at work in the world today. He answers the question—Who will rule the world?—not, How will the world be converted?

The Book of Daniel is the key to understanding other Scriptures. Our Lord, in the Olivet Discourse, quoted only from the Book of Daniel. The Book of Revelation is largely an enigma without the Book of Daniel. Paul's revelation concerning the ". . . man of sin . . ." (2 Thess. 2:3) needs Daniel's account for amplification and clarification.

OUTLINE

I. **The Historic Night with Prophetic Light, Chapters 1—6**
   A. Decline of Judah; Fall of Jerusalem; Daniel Taken Captive to Babylon; His Decision to be True to God, Chapter 1
   B. Dream of Nebuchadnezzar about a Multimetallic Image; Interpretation of Daniel Concerning the Four Kingdoms of "The Times of the Gentiles," Chapter 2
   C. Decree of Nebuchadnezzar to Enforce Universal Idolatry; Three Hebrews Cast into the Furnace for Refusal to Bow to Image of Gold, Chapter 3
   D. Dream of Nebuchadnezzar about a Great Tree Hewn Down to a Stump; Fulfilled in Subsequent Period of Madness of the King, Chapter 4
   E. Downfall of Babylon Foretold by Daniel as He Read the Handwriting on the Wall at the Feast of Belshazzar, Chapter 5
   F. Decree of Darius, the Median, to Enforce Worship of Himself; Daniel Cast into Den of Lions for Praying to the God of Heaven, Chapter 6

II. **The Prophetic Light in the Historic Night, Chapters 7—12**
   A. Daniel's Vision of Four Beasts Concerning Four Kingdoms of "The Times of the Gentiles," Chapter 7
   B. Daniel's Vision of Ram and He Goat and Another Little Horn, Chapter 8
   C. Daniel's Vision of Seventy Weeks Concerning the Nation of Israel, Chapter 9
   D. Daniel's Vision Relating to Israel in Immediate Future and Latter Days; Historical Little Horn and Little Horn of the Latter Days, Chapters 10—12
      1. Preparation for Vision by Prayer of Daniel; Appearance of a Heavenly Messenger, Chapter 10
      2. Prophecy Concerning Persia and Grecia, Historical "Little Horn"; Eschatological "Little Horn," Chapter 11

CHAPTER 1

THEME: *Decline of Judah and fall of Jerusalem; Daniel decides to be true to God; Delight of Nebuchadnezzar in the development of Daniel and his three friends*

DECLINE OF JUDAH AND FALL OF JERUSALEM

In the third year of the reign of Jehoiakim king of Judah came Nebuchadnezzar king of Babylon unto Jerusalem, and besieged it [Dan. 1:1].

Jehoiakim was placed on the throne of Judah by Pharaoh Nechoh to succeed his brother, Jehoahaz. Both of these evil men were sons of Josiah, the godly king who led in the last revival in Judah (see 2 Kings 23:31–37). Jehoiakim's name was actually Eliakim. During his reign Nebuchadnezzar first came against Jerusalem. The year was about 606 B.C.; he took the city in about 604 B.C. The city was not destroyed, but the first group of captives was taken to Babylon. Among these were Daniel, his three friends, and literally thousands of others.

When Jehoiakim died, his son Jehoiachin came to the throne. He rebelled against Nebuchadnezzar who, in 598 B.C., again besieged Jerusalem. Once more Jerusalem was not destroyed, but the king, his mother, and all the vessels of the house of the Lord were taken away to Babylon, along with an even larger group of captives. Evidently among this latter group was Ezekiel (see 2 Kings 24:6–16).

Zedekiah, the uncle of Jehoiachin, was subsequently made king and also rebelled against Nebuchadnezzar. This time Nebuchadnezzar came against the city, destroyed the temple, and burned Jerusalem. The sons of Zedekiah were slain in his presence, and then his own eyes were put out. He, along with the final deportation, went into captivity about 588 or 587 B.C. All this, by the way, was in fulfillment of Jeremiah's prophecy in Jeremiah 25:8–13. Both Jeremiah and Ezekiel had told the people that the false prophets were wrong and that Jerusalem would be destroyed. These two men just happened to have been right.

> **And the Lord gave Jehoiakim king of Judah into his hand, with part of the vessels of the house of God: which he carried into the land of Shinar to the house of his god; and he brought the vessels into the treasure house of his god [Dan. 1:2].**

Only some of the vessels were taken to Babylon at this time; the remainder were removed when Jehoiachin surrendered (see 2 Kings 24:13). Nebuchadnezzar took these vessels and carried them into the land of Shinar to the house of his god. We want to keep this in mind, because later on King Belshazzar (probably a grandson of Nebuchadnezzar) will bring them out for his banquet.

> **And the king spake unto Ashpenaz the master of his eunuchs, that he should bring certain of the children of Israel, and of the king's seed, and of the princes [Dan. 1:3].**

Nebuchadnezzar always took for himself the cream of the crop of the captives from any nation. I think they were given tests to determine their IQ's, and those selected were trained to be wise men to advise the king of Babylon. We will find that Daniel was included in this group and that the king did consult them.

"And the king spake unto Ashpenaz the master of his *eunuchs.*" Verse 9 of this chapter also says: "Now God had brought Daniel into favour and tender love with the prince of the *eunuchs.*" (italics mine) Daniel and his three friends were made eunuchs in fulfillment of Isaiah 39:7, "And of thy sons that shall issue from thee, which thou shalt beget, shall they take away; and they shall be eunuchs in the palace of the king of Babylon."

Most conservative scholars agree that Daniel was taken captive when he was about seventeen years old. He was made a eunuch, and so you can understand why Daniel never married or had any children.

Some people wonder what kind of an oddball Daniel was. Actually, he was no oddball—this was something the king did, and it did not destroy the mental development of these young men. It served the purpose of making them more docile toward the king, and it also enabled them to give all their time to the studies which were given to them. I am sure that it is true today as it was when I was in college: I spent half of my time taking a "course" that was known as dating. I had a lot of good times—I did a great deal of studying, but I could have done lots more! But, you see, the king wanted these boys to spend their time studying, and his way of doing that was to make them eunuchs. Daniel was in this group.

> **Children in whom was no blemish, but well favoured, and skilful in all wisdom, and cunning in knowledge, and understanding science, and such as had ability in them to stand in the king's palace, and whom they might teach the learning and the tongue of the Chaldeans [Dan. 1:4].**

I want to submit to you that the Bible was not written by a bunch of ninnies—it wasn't written by men who were ignorant. Moses was learned in all the wisdom of Egypt. The Egyptians were quite advanced; they knew the distance to the sun, and they knew that the earth was round. It was a few Greeks who came along later and flattened out the earth. They were the "scientists" in that day, you see. Science taught that the earth was flat. The Bible never did teach that; in fact, it said it was a circle (see Isa. 40:22). Daniel, too, as a young man was outstanding. He must have rated high on the list of these young men who were given tests in the court of Nebuchadnezzar. The apostle Paul, who wrote much of the New Testament, was up in that bracket intellectually also. All these were brilliant young men who were exposed to the learning of their day. I get weary of these so-called eggheads who act as if the Bible was written by a group of ignoramuses. If you feel that way about it, you are mistaken. Daniel was nobody's fool. He was a brilliant young man, and he was taught as few men have been taught. Don't despise the learning of that day. There were many men who were well advanced in knowledge, in science, and in many other areas. Daniel is going to be exposed to all that.

> **And the king appointed them a daily provision of the king's meat, and of the wine which he drank: so nourishing them three years, that at the end thereof they might stand before the king [Dan. 1:5].**

"Meat" could be translated "food." This, of course, was the diet of pagans, and it would include unclean animals. Remember that Daniel was a Jew and was under the Mosaic Law. They had been told not to eat certain meats, certain fowl, and certain fish.

DANIEL DECIDES TO BE TRUE TO GOD

> **Now among these were of the children of Judah, Daniel, Hananiah, Mishael, and Azariah:**

> **Unto whom the prince of the eunuchs gave names: for he gave unto Daniel the name of Belteshazzar; and to Hananiah, of Shadrach; and to Mishael, of Meshach; and to Azariah, of Abed-nego [Dan. 1:6–7].**

The prince of the eunuchs actually changes their Hebrew names and gives them pagan names. He gave Daniel the name of *Belteshazzar* which means "worshiper of Baal," a heathen god. He named Hananiah Shadrach, and Mishael Meshach, and Azariah Abed-nego. Notice that the names with which we are acquainted are the heathen names. I think maybe these four boys registered the highest IQ's of the whole group. You see, Babylon wanted the best brains as well as good physical specimens.

These four young men from Judah are singled out and identified to us, and the reason is that they are going to take a stand for God. If all these boys were the same age as Daniel, I would say they were around seventeen years of age. Dr. Arno C. Gaebelein, who was a very able expositor of the Old Testament and especially of the prophetic books, felt that Daniel was about fourteen years old. Sir Robert Anderson gave him the age of around twenty. Therefore, seventeen would be a good conservative estimate of the age of these four.

> **But Daniel purposed in his heart that he would not defile himself with the portion of the king's meat, nor with the wine which he drank: therefore he requested of the prince of the eunuchs that he might not defile himself [Dan. 1:8].**

This boy takes a real stand for God, and he does it in a heathen court. Under normal circumstances, this would have been fatal. Obviously, Daniel was not trying to win a popularity contest. He wasn't attempting to please Nebuchadnezzar. His decision did not reflect the modern softness of compromise which we find all around us today; nor was it dictated by the false philosophies of "How to Win Friends and Influence People" and "The Power of Positive Thinking." Daniel knew nothing of the opportunist's policy of "When In Babylon, do as the Babylonians do." Daniel was not conformed to this world, but he was transformed by the renewing of his mind, and the will of God was the all-absorbing purpose of his life.

Daniel and his friends represented in their day that Jewish remnant which God has had in all ages. This is the remnant of which Paul spoke in Romans 11:5—"Even so then at this present time also there is a remnant according to the election of grace."

Now these boys don't want to eat the king's food; they are going to rebel against a Babylonian diet. Actually, an attempt will be made to brainwash these young men, to make them Babylonians inwardly and outwardly. They were supposed to eat like Babylonians, dress like Babylonians, and think like Babylonians.

However, Daniel and his friends were under the Mosaic system, and God made what they were to eat very clear to His people in the Old Testament. We read in Leviticus 11:44–47: "For I am the LORD your God: ye shall therefore sanctify yourselves, and ye shall be holy; for I am holy: neither shall ye defile yourselves with any manner of creeping thing that creepeth upon the earth. For I am the LORD that bringeth you up out of the land of Egypt, to be your God: ye shall therefore be holy, for I am holy. This is the law of the beasts, and of the fowl, and of every living creature that moveth in the waters, and of every creature that creepeth upon the earth: To make a difference between the unclean and the clean, and between the beast that may be eaten and the beast that may not be eaten." Certain meats were specifically forbidden, and they are listed in the Book of Leviticus; also, meats offered to heathen idols were repulsive to godly Israelites.

Perhaps Daniel and these other Hebrew children were Nazarites to whom even wine was forbidden: "He shall separate himself from wine and strong drink, and shall drink no vinegar of wine, or vinegar of strong drink, neither shall he drink any liquor of grapes, nor eat moist grapes, or dried" (Num. 6:3).

These young men were following the injunction of Isaiah: "Depart ye, depart ye, go ye out from thence, touch no unclean thing; go ye out of the midst of her; be ye clean, that bear the vessels of the LORD" (Isa. 52:11).

However, believers today have not been given a diet chart or menu. Paul tells us in 1 Corinthians 10:25–27: "Whatsoever is sold in the shambles [that is, out yonder in the meat market], that eat, asking no question for conscience sake: For the earth is the Lord's, and the fulness thereof. If any of them that believe not bid you to a feast, and ye be disposed to go; whatsoever is set before you, eat, asking no question for conscience sake." Then again, in 1 Corinthians 8:8, he says, "But meat commendeth us not to God: for neither, if we eat, are we the better; neither, if we eat not, are we the worse."

These Hebrew young men were taking a stand under the Mosaic Law, and they were taking a stand for God.

Now God had brought Daniel into favour and tender love with the prince of the eunuchs [Dan. 1:9].

Now, you see, Daniel is already a favorite, and that is no accident. God was working on Daniel's behalf, even as He worked in the life of Joseph down in the land of Egypt.

**And the prince of the eunuchs said unto Daniel, I fear
my lord the king, who hath appointed your meat and
your drink: for why should he see your faces worse lik-
ing than the children which are of your sort? then shall
ye make me endanger my head to the king [Dan. 1:10].**

The prince of the eunuchs did not want to force the diet upon them,
but he was really on a hot seat. He was caught between a rock and a
hard place. He liked Daniel, but what was he to do?

**Then said Daniel to Melzar whom the prince of the eu-
nuchs had set over Daniel, Hananiah, Mishael, and
Azariah,**

**Prove thy servants, I beseech thee, ten days; and let
them give us pulse to eat, and water to drink [Dan.
1:11–12].**

"Pulse"—some translators have felt that this means vegetables, but I
don't think that is exactly it. Actually, it was a grain they wanted to
eat. To tell the truth, what Daniel was saying was, "Let us have our
pulse, and in a few days we'll show you that we are all right, that we
are in just as good physical condition as the others are."

**Then let our countenances be looked upon before thee,
and the countenance of the children that eat of the portion of the king's meat: and as thou seest, deal with thy
servants [Dan. 1:13].**

In other words: "Test us out, and put us on this diet for a few days to
see if we are not in as good condition as the other fellows are." Well,
God had brought favor from this man Melzar to Daniel, and so Melzar
is going to make the test.

The Bible tells us that Daniel's decision to refuse the Babylonian
diet was something he "purposed in his heart." I want to comment for
a moment on this issue of making Christian living and separation

from the world a matter of a few little rules that have to do with eating and with conduct. There is always a tendency in this area to be dogmatic and forbid certain questionable things, things which are actually debatable.

I received a letter once from a lady who joined a small group shortly after she had become a Christian, and they told her there were certain things she couldn't do and certain things she could do. In the letter which she wrote to me she said, "I have followed all these rules, and yet I am still miserable."

In the history of the church we can see times when people set up a system of doing things and not doing things—systems that actually were *good* at first. For example, the monasteries which began in the Roman Empire were actually a protest against the licentiousness of their day. But before long it was worse on the inside of the monastery than on the outside.

Remember that Christ said to the Pharisees, ". . . Now do ye Pharisees make clean the outside of the cup and the platter; but your inward part is full of ravening and wickedness" (Luke 11:39). In other words, "You make the outside of the cup clean, but inside it's dirty. It is just like whitewashing a tomb." Today it is "Not by works of righteousness which we have done, but according to his mercy he saved us, by the washing of regeneration, and renewing of the Holy Ghost" (Titus 3:5). In order to live a life of holiness, we must first receive new life from God—we must be born from above.

"Daniel purposed in his heart" (v. 8)—it all began in the heart of Daniel. He was not a papier-mâché; he had a heart, and his convictions came from his heart. That should be our experience also. We are captives in this world in which we live; gravitation holds all of us by the seat of our pants, and we cannot jump off this earth. The Lord Jesus said that we are in the world, but not of the world. And He said, ". . . Ye cannot serve God and mammon" (Matt. 6:24). However, we cannot serve God by following a set of rules; we must have a purpose in our hearts. Jesus said that it was out of the heart that the issues of life proceed; the things which we put into our bodies are not the most important. Daniel purposed in his heart that he would obey God's law given to God's people Israel—this was to be his testimony.

So he consented to them in this matter, and proved them ten days [Dan. 1:14].

The prince of the eunuchs was rather reluctant to go along with Daniel's suggestion because he had been brought up in Babylonian culture and believed that this diet was the thing which produced geniuses. However, he liked Daniel and gave them ten days to test it out.

DELIGHT OF NEBUCHADNEZZAR IN THE DEVELOPMENT OF DANIEL AND HIS THREE FRIENDS

And at the end of ten days their countenances appeared fairer and fatter in flesh than all the children which did eat the portion of the king's meat [Dan. 1:15].

Daniel's diet worked in their behalf. This ought to tell us something. God wanted His people Israel to be different from the surrounding nations, but He did not give them a special diet just to make them different—there was also a health factor involved. I firmly believe that if we followed the diet outlined in Leviticus, we would be healthier than our neighbor who eats just anything. But we can eat anything we want; we are not under the law. I have found, though, that it is a matter of health. I have had a number of physical problems and have discovered, among other things, that pork just isn't the best thing for us. Israel's God-given diet was very meaningful healthwise, and it had more than just a ceremonial basis.

Thus Melzar took away the portion of their meat, and the wine that they should drink; and gave them pulse.

As for these four children, God gave them knowledge and skill in all learning and wisdom: and Daniel had understanding in all visions and dreams [Dan. 1:16–17].

Just as God blessed Solomon, God is blessing these Hebrew children who were in a foreign court. Daniel will eventually become prime minister to two great world empires.

"Daniel had understanding in all visions and dreams." Daniel was still in the time of revelation, the time in which God used dreams and visions. Now don't you say that God has spoken to you in a dream, because I must contradict you. I do not think that God is speaking to us that way—He speaks to us today in His Word.

For a great many people it is easier to dream about the Word than it is to study it. I used to have students in a Bible institute who would very piously pray the night before an exam. They didn't study much, but they were very pious about it all. One student told me that he stuck his Bible under his pillow the night before an examination! I asked him, "Do you really think the names of the kings of Israel and Judah will come up through the duck feathers and get into your brain?" The Holy Spirit is not a help and a crutch for a lazy person. You are going to have to study the Word of God. God speaks to us through His written Word today.

However, God is speaking audibly to Daniel, for he is now writing one of the books of the Bible. In spite of what the critics say, Daniel wrote it—it was not written three or four hundred years later.

Now at the end of the days that the king had said he should bring them in, then the prince of the eunuchs brought them in before Nebuchadnezzar [Dan. 1:18].

Nebuchadnezzar is going to look at the training which was given to them to see if it has been the proper training. I honestly believe the Communists have been very stupid in their methods of brainwashing. They attempt to break a man down. You can break down any human being; he will finally give in, of course. A man can only take so much. But this man Nebuchadnezzar really knew how to do it. He gave them a lot of food, he tested them, and finally he placed them in a fine position. He did all this in a friendly way. This was his philosophy, his way of making friends and influencing people.

> And the king communed with them; and among them
> all was found none like Daniel, Hananiah, Mishael, and
> Azariah: therefore stood they before the king [Dan.
> 1:19].

Nebuchadnezzar talked with those four boys and found they were geniuses, and so he gave them good positions in his kingdom.

> And in all matters of wisdom and understanding, that
> the king inquired of them, he found them ten times bet-
> ter than all the magicians and astrologers that were in
> all his realm [Dan. 1:20].

Daniel is moved to the head of the class.

> And Daniel continued even unto the first year of king
> Cyrus [Dan. 1:21].

With verse 1 and this verse we can learn Daniel's life span. Coming to
Babylon at about the age of seventeen, he died when he was about
ninety years of age. He bridged the entire seventy years of captivity.
He did not return to Israel but apparently died before the people left
Babylon. We actually have no record about that.

CHAPTER 2

THEME: The dream of Nebuchadnezzar about a multi-metallic image; the interpretation of Daniel concerning the four kingdoms of "the times of the Gentiles"

We are in one of the great sections of the Word of God as far as prophecy is concerned. The multimetallic image (ch. 2), the four beasts (ch. 7), and the seventy weeks of Daniel (ch. 9) form the backbone and ribs of biblical prophecy. You could never have a skeleton of prophecy without these passages of Scripture in the Old Testament.

Everything the Lord Jesus said in the Olivet Discourse was based on the Book of Daniel. The disciples asked Him, ". . . Tell us, when shall these things be? and what shall be the sign of thy coming, and of the end of the world?" He replied, "When ye therefore shall see the abomination of desolation, spoken of by Daniel the prophet . . ." (Matt. 24:3, 15). This chapter, then, is a very important chapter in the Word of God.

Men everywhere are asking, "What is this world coming to? How are things going to be worked out today? There are crises everywhere." My friend, the times of the Gentiles are going to run out. The gentiles have not done a very good job of running the world. We can see the beginning of that way back in the Book of Daniel, and we may come close to seeing the end of it. However, the church of Jesus Christ will leave this earth before the fullness of the Gentiles comes in; and, when the church leaves, Christ will come back to the earth to rule.

This prophetic chapter is basic to the understanding of all prophecy. That is why I keep insisting that to know just a few little verses of Scripture and to be able to interpret them can be a dangerous thing. This is the way the cults begin: they use only certain verses of Scripture. The men who start these cults understand history and human nature; they know man's need for a doctrine which satisfies the natural mind. Liberalism and the social gospel appeal to the natural mind.

A young preacher in the East told me of a minister in a neighboring town who was building a great empire of his church. Yet that man drinks and curses and goes out with the boys, probably doing everything else the boys do. The young preacher asked me, "How is that man drawing people to his church? They come to hear him and to join his church—not mine. But I am attempting to preach the Word of God!" I told that young man that we need to realize that if we are going to represent God in the ministry, we are going to be in the minority. The other minister was appealing to the natural mind. He may have baptized many—he may have got them under the water and got a lot of water on them—but he had not led people to a saving knowledge of Christ.

Saint Augustine, who became a great man of God, was asked why he had succumbed earlier to the Manichean heresy of his day. He replied that it was "so complete and reasonable." The philosophical approach used by so many preachers today is probably the most dangerous approach to the Word of God that is imaginable. They never think to go to the Word of God as the foundation and the authority. Rather, they want to give you the interpretation of some man of the past, such as Plato. When I was preparing to enter the ministry, that is the direction I wanted to take because it appeals to people and it shows how smart you are. Thank God that I got under the assistance and influence of two men who put me on the track of simply teaching the Bible, letting the chips fall where they may. It is so important to study the entire Word of God, and therefore this section is important to us.

THE DREAM OF NEBUCHADNEZZAR AND HIS DEMANDS UPON THE WISE MEN OF BABYLON

And in the second year of the reign of Nebuchadnezzar, Nebuchadnezzar dreamed dreams, wherewith his spirit was troubled, and his sleep brake from him [Dan. 2:1].

I am confident that Nebuchadnezzar, who had now been lifted and exalted to a very high position, wondered about this great empire that

had come into existence under his leadership. Actually, Babylon was
the first great world empire. Nebuchadnezzar had done something
that the Egyptians had not been able to do because Egypt was self-
contained. The biggest mistake any pharaoh ever made was to leave
the Nile River. If he just stayed there, he was well protected—he had a
wall of desert around him which nobody could breach. All he needed
to do was guard the Nile River which was the only entrance into
Egypt. The Egyptians began to reach out, but they never did become
what you would call a world empire, although they did influence the
world as few nations have.

However, this man Nebuchadnezzar began as a petty chieftain and
united several tribes. Then he took over the Assyrian Empire, then the
Syrian, and he was on the march. And he overcame the Egyptians.
The Greeks would have been unable to offer resistance, but he made
no effort to move in their direction. He didn't need to, as he was actually ruling the then-known world. Nebuchadnezzar had to think this
thing over, and when he did, he found he had a world empire on his
hands. It was sort of like the old bromide about getting a lion by the
tail—you can't hold on and you can't turn him loose. That is the position Nebuchadnezzar was in, and God spoke to him at that time.

This man was troubled in his sleep, wondering about the future of
this great empire he had founded: Where was it all going to end? Do
you know that after about 2500 years of human history since Nebuchadnezzar we are still wondering about that? We have the answer
here in this chapter, by the way.

> **Then the king commanded to call the magicians, and
> the astrologers, and the sorcerers, and the Chaldeans,
> for to shew the king his dreams. So they came and stood
> before the king [Dan. 2:2].**

Nebuchadnezzar called in all his wise men. These were the men who
had been trained even as Daniel and his friends had been trained.
They were the old boys who were called in for this conference. In
other words, the king summoned his cabinet.

These wise men were men of great intellect and learning. It is true that they held many superstitions and concepts of a heathen religion, but, my friend, I don't know how much farther we've come today. I know some Ph.D.'s who reject the Bible—I think they are heathen and a little superstitious, by the way. Isn't it interesting that the Bible has been ruled out of our schools; yet they are teaching astrology and all kinds of superstitions which have been rejected by civilized people in the past. Don't look down on the wise men of Babylon—they are just as smart as some of our Ph.D.'s and Th.D.'s today.

These men comprised the brain trust of Babylon, and they were brought before the king to hear his unique command:

> **And the king said unto them, I have dreamed a dream, and my spirit was troubled to know the dream [Dan. 2:3].**

The king explains that he has had an unusual dream which he believes to have some far-reaching significance. You see, God made it clear to him that He had something to say, but this man in his darkness knew only that it was something important.

> **Then spake the Chaldeans to the king in Syriac, O king, live for ever: tell thy servants the dream, and we will shew the interpretation [Dan. 2:4].**

"Then spake the Chaldeans to the king in Syriac, O king, live for ever." To me that seems to be about the silliest thing they could ever say, but that was the way they flattered the king—"O king, live for ever." I am sure that many a king who sat there on the throne had a heart condition and might well have said, "Well, boys, you are wrong. I'm not going to live forever. I'm going to have a heart attack one of these days, and I won't be around." However, they seem to have avoided that issue.

It is important to note that at this juncture in the Book of Daniel there is a change from the Hebrew to the Aramaic or Syriac language, as it is called here in verse 4. From verse 4 of this chapter through verse 28 of chapter 7, the book is written in Aramaic or Syriac. Aramaic was the court language, the diplomatic language of that day. It was the language of the Gentiles, the language of the world. It would correspond to what French was a few years ago; today I think English is the language that has supplanted French in that position.

The significance of this change is quite remarkable: God is now speaking to *the world*, not just to His nation. Israel has gone into Babylonian captivity. God has taken the scepter out of the line of David, and He has put it in gentile hands. It will stay there until the day He takes the scepter back. When He does, nail-pierced hands will take the scepter, because it is God's intention for Jesus to reign.

The subject here is a worldwide kingdom. The idea that the Word of God is confined to some local deity and that the Bible has quite a limited view is entirely wrong. If we examine it carefully, we find that God has in mind a worldwide kingdom. In Psalm 89:27 He says of the covenant He made with David: "Also I will make him my firstborn, higher than the kings of the earth." Then in verses 34–37 of the same psalm He says: "My covenant will I not break, nor alter the thing that is gone out of my lips. Once have I sworn by my holiness that I will not lie unto David. His seed shall endure for ever, and his throne as the sun before me. It shall be established for ever as the moon, and as a faithful witness in heaven." In other words, God is saying, "If you can go out and see that the sun has disappeared from the heaven and the moon is not out at night, then you will know that I have changed My mind; but as long as you see the sun and moon, you will know that I am going to put My king over this earth."

We are talking now about that which is global and not some local situation. This concerns the first great world ruler, and the language used is the language of the world of that day.

The king answered and said to the Chaldeans, The thing is gone from me: if ye will not make known unto me the dream, with the interpretation thereof, ye shall be cut in pieces, and your houses shall be made a dunghill [Dan. 2:5].

This would be a rather extreme judgment, but you can see what the king wants. Frankly, a faulty translation of this verse gives the impression that the king had forgotten his dream. He hadn't forgotten his dream. He knows the dream, senses its importance, and refuses to divulge it to the wise men. Why? He wants to get a correct interpretation of it. In the margin, the American Standard Version of 1901 translates "The thing is gone from me" as, "The word is gone forth from me." In other words, Nebuchadnezzar is saying to these men, "I will not change my mind about this judgment I am pronouncing. Don't beg me to tell you the dream—I'm not going to do it. You are going to come up with the dream if I am to listen to your interpretation of it." The Berkeley Version has a helpful translation at this point also: "The king answered the Chaldeans, 'This word I speak, I mean! If you do not tell me the dream and what it means, you shall be torn limb from limb and your houses will be destroyed.'" That translation really tones it down, but nevertheless the penalty is still excessive and extreme. Nebuchadnezzar is putting fear in these men. They have to come up with the interpretation of the dream, but they first of all have to give what the dream was.

> **But if ye shew the dream, and the interpretation thereof, ye shall receive of me gifts and rewards and great honour: therefore shew me the dream, and the interpretation thereof [Dan. 2:6].**

Conversely, Nebuchadnezzar could be generous and charitable. This man was greatly governed by his emotions, as we are going to see. He tells them, "I am going to amply reward you if you give me the correct interpretation."

> **They answered again and said, Let the king tell his servants the dream, and we will shew the interpretation of it [Dan. 2:7].**

The wise men realized their dangerous predicament, and they again cautiously suggest to the king that he supply the dream and they will supply the interpretation.

> **The king answered and said, I know of certainty that ye
> would gain the time, because ye see the thing is gone
> from me [Dan. 2:8].**

The king says, "You see that I mean business and so you are stalling.
You want a little more time." The Berkeley Version clarifies this verse:
"The king replied, 'I see plainly that you are trying to gain time; because you see how capital punishment awaits you.'" That is taking a
little liberty with the translation, but that actually is the meaning of it.

> **But if ye will not make known unto me the dream, there
> is but one decree for you: for ye have prepared lying and
> corrupt words to speak before me, till the time be
> changed: therefore tell me the dream, and I shall know
> that ye can shew me the interpretation thereof [Dan.
> 2:9].**

The king really reveals here his lack of confidence in the wise men of
Babylon. I think they probably had failed him on previous assign-
ments, just as the prophets of Baal failed old Ahab (but since Ahab
died in battle, he didn't have a chance to retaliate). Nebuchadnezzar
feels these men have been feeding him a great deal of malarkey, and he
is now putting them to a real test. His reasoning at this point is very
logical: If they can tell him his dream, then it is reasonable to conclude that their interpretation is genuine. If they cannot tell him his
dream, any interpretation would be under suspicion.

DECREE TO DESTROY THE WISE MEN FOR THEIR FAILURE

> **The Chaldeans answered before the king, and said,
> There is not a man upon the earth that can shew the
> king's matter: therefore there is no king, lord, nor ruler,
> that asked such things at any magician, or astrologer, or
> Chaldean [Dan. 2:10].**

This is the first true statement the wise men have made—no man on earth could give the dream, only God could. In desperation they are pleading for their lives, trying to show the unreasonableness of the king's demand. If you leave out the supernatural, of course his demands are unreasonable. However, they have made claim to be superior, and he is asking them to demonstrate that.

> **And it is a rare thing that the king requireth, and there is none other that can shew it before the king, except the gods, whose dwelling is not with flesh [Dan. 2:11].**

What they are saying is that they have no communication with heaven. They even confessed that their gods were not giving them very much information. They conclude their argument by saying that no human being could meet the king's demands. This paves the way for Daniel to come onto the scene.

> **For this cause the king was angry and very furious, and commanded to destroy all the wise men of Babylon [Dan. 2:12].**

The king exhibits here a violent temper for which he was noted. It is another symptom of the psychosis he is suffering and which we will see later on. The king orders the wise men to be destroyed summarily.

> **And the decree went forth that the wise men should be slain; and they sought Daniel and his fellows to be slain [Dan. 2:13].**

The king's decree includes Daniel and his brethren. Although they are just being trained, they are being taught by the same crowd in which the king has now lost confidence. The rash order to destroy the wise men of Babylon is going to take in a great many men who were really innocent and who could not be held responsible. The dictatorship of

Nebuchadnezzar could be carried to the *nth* degree—he could do what he wanted to.

DANIEL'S DESIRE TO TELL THE DREAM

Then Daniel answered with counsel and wisdom to Arioch the captain of the king's guard, which was gone forth to slay the wise men of Babylon:

He answered and said to Arioch the king's captain, Why is the decree so hasty from the king? Then Arioch made the thing known to Daniel [Dan. 2:14–15].

Daniel is really puzzled at the hasty and unjust decree of the king, but he uses tact as he approaches Arioch. Arioch is the captain of the king's guard—he is in charge of the Secret Service of that day—and, naturally, is often in the presence of the king. It would be interesting to know all that Arioch communicated to Daniel. I wonder if he suggested to Daniel that the king was off his rocker or that the king didn't have all his marbles. It is not recorded here if he did, but I think he touched his head and said, "You know how the king is!"

Then Daniel went in, and desired of the king that he would give him time, and that he would shew the king the interpretation [Dan. 2:16].

Daniel got an audience with the king—he is already in favor—and he requested the king to give him time to tell him the dream. This seems presumptuous; in fact, it seems to be the act of a very brash young man. However, succeeding events will reveal that it was the confidence of a man with faith in God.

Then Daniel went to his house, and made the thing known to Hananiah, Mishael, and Azariah, his companions:

That they would desire mercies of the God of heaven concerning this secret; that Daniel and his fellows

should not perish with the rest of the wise men of Babylon [Dan. 2:17–18].

"That they would desire mercies of *the God of heaven*." This is an expression which you will find only in the books of the captivity, including Ezra, Nehemiah, and Daniel. You see, after the departure of the glory of God from Jerusalem, from the Holy of Holies in the temple, He was addressed as "the God of heaven." These Hebrew young men knew that God did not dwell in some little temple in Jerusalem. He is "the God of heaven."

"That they would desire *mercies*" reveals the basis of their prayers. God does not answer prayer because of the worth or the effort or the character or the works of the one who is praying. All prayer must rest upon His mercy. To pray today in Jesus' name simply means that we come to God, not on our merit, but on His merit, looking to Him for mercy.

DANIEL DESCRIBES THE DREAM
AS A MULTIMETALLIC IMAGE

Then was the secret revealed unto Daniel in a night vision. Then Daniel blessed the God of heaven [Dan. 2:19].

I would think that the way God revealed this to Daniel was to give him the same dream He gave to Nebuchadnezzar. This would seem to be the reasonable explanation.

Daniel answered and said, Blessed be the name of God for ever and ever: for wisdom and might are his:

And he changeth the times and the seasons: he removeth kings, and setteth up kings: he giveth wisdom unto the wise, and knowledge to them that know understanding:

He revealeth the deep and secret things: he knoweth what is in the darkness, and the light dwelleth with him.

I thank thee, and praise thee, O thou God of my fathers, who hast given me wisdom and might, and hast made known unto me now what we desired of thee: for thou hast now made known unto us the king's matter [Dan. 2:20–23].

This is one of the several recorded prayers of Daniel. Daniel was a man of purpose, a man of prayer, and a man of prophecy. God alone has revealed this secret to Daniel, and this is his tremendous prayer of thanksgiving. Now Daniel is ready to go in and ask again for an audience with the king.

Therefore Daniel went in unto Arioch, whom the king had ordained to destroy the wise men of Babylon: he went and said thus unto him, Destroy not the wise men of Babylon: bring me in before the king, and I will shew unto the king the interpretation [Dan. 2:24].

Daniel wants to stop the bloody slaughter that would have taken place, and apparently Arioch has no heart for the matter either—he doesn't want to slay all the wise men.

Then Arioch brought in Daniel before the king in haste, and said thus unto him, I have found a man of the captives of Judah, that will make known unto the king the interpretation [Dan. 2:25].

Arioch rushes Daniel into the presence of the king with the good news that the dream will be divulged.

The king answered and said to Daniel, whose name was Belteshazzar, Art thou able to make known unto me the

**dream which I have seen, and the interpretation
thereof? [Dan. 2:26].**

Quite obviously and, I think, logically, the king was rather skeptical.
All of these wise men had not been able to come up with the dream
and its interpretation, but here comes this young fellow Daniel who
says he will be able to. The king asks him, "Do you mean to tell me
that all the other wise men had no answer, but you think you can answer me? Maybe this is just another attempt of the wise men to stall
for time!" His question sounds rather cynical, but Daniel has a marvelous answer for him:

> **Daniel answered in the presence of the king, and said,
> The secret which the king hath demanded cannot the
> wise men, the astrologers, the magicians, the sooth-
> sayers, shew unto the king;**
>
> **But there is a God in heaven that revealeth secrets, and
> maketh known to the king Nebuchadnezzar what shall
> be in the latter days. Thy dream, and the visions of thy
> head upon thy bed, are these [Dan. 2:27–28].**

Daniel immediately makes a distinction between the wisdom of Babylon and the wisdom of God. The apostle Paul wrote, ". . . hath not
God made foolish the wisdom of this world?" and also, ". . . the foolishness of God is wiser than men; and the weakness of God is stronger
than men" (1 Cor. 1:20, 25).

Daniel now has the unique privilege of introducing to the dark-
ened mind of this pagan king the living and true God. He says, "There
is a God in heaven that revealeth secrets, and maketh known to the
king Nebuchadnezzar *what shall be in the latter days.*" This is very
important because it is going to be the emphasis in the Book of Daniel;
this dream refers to the end of the times of the Gentiles.

The end of "the times of the Gentiles" runs concurrently with "the
latter days" of the nation Israel: both come to their fulfillment during
the Great Tribulation period. The day in which you and I live is

"man's day." Paul said in 1 Corinthians 4:3, "But with me it is a very small thing that I should be judged of you, or of man's judgment [day]: yea, I judge not mine own self." We are living in the day of man.

It is also well to note that the term, "the times of the Gentiles," is not synonymous with the term, "the fulness of the Gentiles." Romans 11:25 says, "For I would not, brethren, that ye should be ignorant of this mystery, lest ye should be wise in your own conceits; that blindness in part is happened to Israel, until the fulness of the Gentiles be come in." The fulness of the Gentiles ends with the Rapture of the church. The terms, "the latter days" and "the times of the Gentiles," are not synonymous with "the last days" of the church which come to a fulfillment at the Rapture and precede the Great Tribulation. "The times of the Gentiles" will continue right on into the Great Tribulation, and at that time God will again turn His attention back to the nation Israel.

> **As for thee, O king, thy thoughts came into thy mind upon thy bed, what should come to pass hereafter: and he that revealeth secrets maketh known to thee what shall come to pass [Dan. 2:29].**

Nebuchadnezzar was bothered as he lay in bed at night, wondering what the future held. Although he started out as a petty king, he now finds himself a world ruler.

> **But as for me, this secret is not revealed to me for any wisdom that I have more than any living, but for their sakes that shall make known the interpretation to the king, and that thou mightest know the thoughts of thy heart [Dan. 2:30].**

The dream had to do with the future of Nebuchadnezzar's kingdom and the outcome of his great world empire. Nebuchadnezzar was troubled about the future of this empire of which he suddenly found himself the possessor and dictator. The dream was God's answer to his problem.

Daniel makes it clear that he himself deserves no credit, that God in heaven had revealed the dream, that God was prompted to reveal the dream to spare the lives of the wise men as well as to satisfy the curiosity of this man Nebuchadnezzar.

God is going to speak to Nebuchadnezzar in a language that he will understand, the language of the outward splendor and glory of his kingdom. In the dream God showed him the outward splendor of his kingdom. This dream was also the dream of a Gentile, and in it God spoke to him by using an image. The image in Nebuchadnezzar's dream was not an image to be worshiped; but, because Nebuchadnezzar did fall down before images in the city of Babylon, God used an image in his dream. In this land of idolatry, such a vision was the only language Nebuchadnezzar could truly understand. Babylon was known as the fountainhead of pagan religion, the womb of heathen idols.

We will see in this section the history of the rule of this world by the Gentiles. Because of the failure of the house of David, God is now taking the scepter of this universe out from the hands of that line of David, and He is putting it in the hands of the Gentiles. It will be there until Jesus Christ comes again to this earth. Then Christ will take the scepter and rule on this earth as King of kings and Lord of lords. "The times of the Gentiles" is from the day of Nebuchadnezzar right on down through our day until the Lord comes to reign.

Thou, O king, sawest, and behold a great image. This great image, whose brightness was excellent, stood before thee; and the form thereof was terrible [Dan. 2:31].

That is, the image excited terror—it was awe-inspiring. It was very glamorous, terrific, and stupendous. As Daniel began to describe the dream, I wish that I could have been there to see the expression on Nebuchadnezzar's face change from cynicism to unconcealed amazement. When Daniel began to say, "You saw a great image, the brightness of which was terrific and stupendous," I think the eyes of Nebuchadnezzar lighted up. He shifted to the edge of his throne and said, "Boy, that's it! You are starting out right!"

This image's head was of fine gold, his breast and his arms of silver, his belly and his thighs of brass,

His legs of iron, his feet part of iron and part of clay [Dan. 2:32–33].

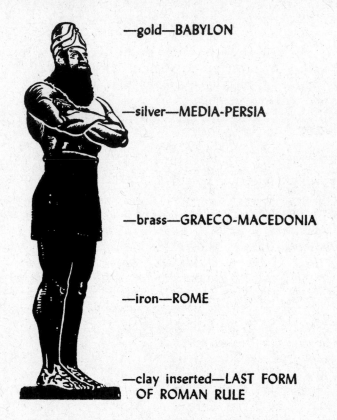

—gold—BABYLON

—silver—MEDIA-PERSIA

—brass—GRAECO-MACEDONIA

—iron—ROME

—clay inserted—LAST FORM OF ROMAN RULE

When Daniel said this, I think the king again said, "Boy, you are exactly right!" Now Nebuchadnezzar is prepared to listen to the interpretation. Tregelles has said of this dream: "Here all is presented as set before the king according to his ability of apprehension—the external and visible things being shown as man might regard them." As we have said, God is speaking to him in a language that he can understand.

This tremendous image that is before him just stands there. There is no movement at all. It is simply awe-inspiring, glamorous, terrific, and stupendous. The head was of gold, the breast and arms of silver, the belly and thighs of brass, the legs of iron, and the feet were iron and clay mixed together. The image therefore consisted of a very strange assortment of metals. It was not an alloy of metals, but a multi-metallic image of four metals plus a silicon (that is, sand or clay).

> **Thou sawest till that a stone was cut out without hands, which smote the image upon his feet that were of iron and clay, and brake them to pieces.**

> **Then was the iron, the clay, the brass, the silver, and the gold, broken to pieces together, and became like the chaff of the summer threshingfloors; and the wind carried them away, that no place was found for them: and the stone that smote the image became a great mountain, and filled the whole earth [Dan. 2:34–35].**

We will get the interpretation of this later on. We will let Daniel give the interpretation—we do not need to guess about it at all. The thing to note here is that, as Nebuchadnezzar beheld the image in awe and wonder, the stone, coming from beyond the environs of the image and without human origin or motivation, smote the image on the feet of iron and clay with such force that all the metals were pulverized. Then a wind blew the dust of the image away, so that it entirely disappeared. Then the stone began to grow as a living stone, and it filled the whole world, taking the place of this image.

DEFINITION OF FOUR WORLD EMPIRES AND THEIR DESTINIES

> **This is the dream; and we will tell the interpretation thereof before the king.**

Thou, O king, art a king of kings: for the God of heaven hath given thee a kingdom, power, and strength, and glory.

And wheresoever the children of men dwell, the beasts of the field and the fowls of the heaven hath he given into thine hand, and hath made thee ruler over them all. Thou art this head of gold [Dan. 2:36–38].

Nebuchadnezzar was the first great world ruler. I think that this was God's ideal for Adam—he was given dominion, but he lost it. The world has known four great world rulers; there have been four great nations who have attempted to rule the world. They all just butchered the job—none of them made a real success of it—but the first one, Nebuchadnezzar, did the best job.

Daniel immediately began to interpret the dream. The different metals represent world empires. Nebuchadnezzar is identified as the head of gold. He exercised rulership over the then-known world. No one questioned his authority. His was an absolute monarchy, and there have been very few since then, by the way. More is said about this Babylonian empire in other sections of the Bible, including Daniel 5:18–19 and Jeremiah 27:5–11. Through Jeremiah God said: "I have made the earth, the man and the beast that are upon the ground, by my great power and by my outstretched arm, and have given it unto whom it seemed meet unto me. And now have I given all these lands into the hand of Nebuchadnezzar the king of Babylon, my servant; and the beasts of the field have I given him also to serve him. And all nations shall serve him, and his son, and his son's son, until the very time of his land come . . ." (Jer. 27:5–7). God made Nebuchadnezzar the one at the top; He made him the first great world ruler, and there has been none like him since then.

And after thee shall arise another kingdom inferior to thee, and another third kingdom of brass, which shall bear rule over all the earth [Dan. 2:39].

The kingdom which will come after Nebuchadnezzar will be inferior to his. The third one will be inferior to the second, and the fourth will be inferior to the third. That means the fourth one is the worst form of all. That is where we are today.

There are two kingdoms mentioned in this verse. The arms of silver represent Media and Persia. In Daniel 5:28 we are told the future of the Babylonian kingdom: "Thy kingdom is divided, and given to the Medes and Persians." We don't need to speculate as to who the second kingdom is—it is made clear. Remember that Daniel lived in both the kingdom of Nebuchadnezzar and the kingdom of Media-Persia. We read in Daniel 6:8, "Now, O king, establish the decree, and sign the writing, that it be not changed, according to the law of the Medes and Persians, which altereth not."

The third kingdom would be a kingdom of brass and would "bear rule over all the earth." This is the Graeco-Macedonian Empire of Alexander the Great.

This brings us to the fourth kingdom. It is important to note that there are only four—there is no fifth kingdom. The period of the fourth kingdom is where we are today.

> **And the fourth kingdom shall be strong as iron: forasmuch as iron breaketh in pieces and subdueth all things: and as iron that breaketh all these, shall it break in pieces and bruise.**
>
> **And whereas thou sawest the feet and toes, part of potters' clay, and part of iron, the kingdom shall be divided; but there shall be in it of the strength of the iron, forasmuch as thou sawest the iron mixed with miry clay.**
>
> **And as the toes of the feet were part of iron, and part of clay, so the kingdom shall be partly strong, and partly broken.**
>
> **And whereas thou sawest iron mixed with miry clay, they shall mingle themselves with the seed of men: but they shall not cleave one to another, even as iron is not mixed with clay [Dan. 2:40–43].**

This is a remarkable passage of Scripture. More attention is directed to this fourth kingdom than to the other three kingdoms put together. Four verses are used here by Daniel to describe it and interpret it. Only one verse, verse 39, is used to describe the second and third kingdoms, the Medo-Persian and the Graeco-Macedonian empires.

The fourth kingdom is the kingdom of the latter days. Remember that Daniel had told Nebuchadnezzar that that was the reason for the image. God is speaking to Nebuchadnezzar, an idol worshiper, through this image, and He is telling Nebuchadnezzar what shall be in the latter days. He is a world ruler, and he is concerned about where it is all going to end. My friend, we are living in the period of the latter days, and that is still the question today: What is this world coming to?

We need to stand back and look at this image again for a moment. It is awe-inspiring and of tremendous size. I think it towered over the entire plain of Babylon as Nebuchadnezzar saw it in his vision. It is a multimetallic image. It has a head of gold, and that speaks of Babylon. The breast and arms are of silver—Medo-Persia. The brass is Graeco-Macedonia. The legs are of iron, and that is Rome. In the feet, clay is inserted into the iron, which is the last form of the Roman Empire.

The image represents four empires, and there are several observations to be made about them. There is a definite deterioration from one kingdom to another, and this is made clear in several very specific ways. This deterioration is contrary to modern philosophy and opinion. Our viewpoint today is that we are all getting better and better every day: evolution is at work, and it is onward and upward forever. We feel that we have the best form of government and that we are superior people—neither of which is true. The human race has always liked to pat itself on the back as Little Jack Horner did:

> Little Jack Horner
> Sat in the corner,
> Eating of Christmas pie:
> He put in his thumb,
> And pulled out a plum,
> And said, "What a good boy am I!"

However, what we have here is the *deterioration* from one kingdom to the other—each is inferior to its predecessor. This is revealed through the image in several ways:

1. The *quality* of the metals: gold is finer than silver, and silver is finer that brass. Brass is finer than iron, and iron is better than clay. There is definite deterioration.

2. The *specific gravity* of the metals: each metal shows deterioration; Tregelles (as quoted by Culver) is the scholar who called attention to this factor.

3. The *position* of each metal: the head has more honor than do the feet.

4. The specific *statement of* Scripture: "And after thee shall arise another kingdom inferior to thee" (v. 39). Scripture is clear that each kingdom is to be inferior to the one before it.

5. The *division of sovereignty:* the definite division of sovereignty denotes weakness. Nebuchadnezzar is the head of gold, but there are two arms of the Medo-Persian Empire. The Babylonian Empire was strong because there was not that division. The Graeco-Macedonian Empire begins with one, but soon is divided into four. Rome has two legs of iron, but it eventuates into ten toes which are composed of both iron and clay.

In the United States today we like to believe we have the very best form of government, and people eagerly say they "believe in democracy." Actually, our form of government is not a democracy, but a representative form of government. No one asks me to come to Washington, D.C., to make any decisions. There are many who do go to Washington to tell them how to do it, and I think somebody needs to tell them. The problem is that it is the wrong people who are doing the telling. I am of the opinion that a democracy is really not the best form of government.

God's form of government is going to be just exactly like that head of gold, only the ruler will be that Rock that is "cut out without hands"—none other than the Lord Jesus Christ. He is going to reign over this earth, and He is not going to ask anybody for advice about it. He will not have a Congress, and He will not have a Cabinet, and He will not be calling upon you to vote for Him. In fact, if you don't make a decision for Him in this life, my friend, you just won't be there at all. Don't rebel against that fact, because this happens to be His world— He created it. You and I are just little pygmies running around down here. God has as much right to remove you and me from this little world as I have to remove those ants that get into my house and yard. I set out poison for those fellows—I want to get rid of them. Why? Because they don't fit into my program. There are a lot of us who don't fit into God's program. This is His world, and He is going to make it to suit Himself.

God's form of government is going to be one of the most strict forms of government that the world has ever seen. I do not think a rooster is going to crow in that day without His permission to do so. The Lord Jesus Christ is going to be a dictator, and if you are not willing to bow to Him, I don't think you would even want to be in His Kingdom when He establishes it here upon the earth. Maybe it is good that He has another place for folk like that, because it will not be pleasant for them to be here—they wouldn't enjoy it at all. God's form of government is the absolute rule of a king, the sovereignty of one ruler. It is going to be autocratic, dictatorial, and His will is going to prevail. That is the reason it is well for you and me to practice bowing to Him and acknowledging Him. He is going to take over one of these days.

Before we move on, we need to notice one more thing: No great world power follows Rome. The Roman Empire is the last, and it will be in existence in the latter days. Actually, it exists today. All of these other empires were destroyed by an enemy from the outside, but no enemy destroyed Rome. Attila the Hun came in and sacked the city, but he was so awestruck by what he saw that he realized he could not handle it. He took his barbarians and left town. The Roman Empire fell apart from within—no enemy destroyed it. Rome is living in the great nations of Europe today: Italy, France, Great Britain, Germany, and Spain are all part of the old Roman Empire. The laws of Rome live on, and her language also. No one speaks Latin today, but it is basic to understanding French, Spanish, and other languages. Her warlike spirit lives on also: Europe has been at war ever since the empire broke up into these kingdoms.

What is happening in Europe today? There is a new psychological viewpoint developing. The young people there do not want to be called Italians or Germans; they like to be called Europeans. Such thinking is creating a basis for the man who is coming someday to put the Roman Empire back together again. He is known in Scripture as the Man of Sin, or the Antichrist. They have a Common Market in Europe today, and they may be well along in restoring the Roman Empire. But not until God takes down the roadblock will that man appear and all this come to fruition. Because he is Satan's man, God will not let him appear until He has called out His people to His name. When He has done that, He will remove His church from the earth. God *is* carrying out His program whether it looks like it or not.

Therefore, there is one coming who will put the Roman Empire together again. I never speak of the *resurrection* of the Roman Empire; that implies that it died. Let me again quote a nursery rhyme:

> Humpty-Dumpty sat on a wall,
> Humpty-Dumpty had a great fall;
> All the King's horses, and all the King's men
> Could not put Humpty-Dumpty together again.

You see, the Roman Empire fell apart like Humpty-Dumpty. There have been a lot of men who tried to put it together again, but they have not succeeded. That was one of the missions of the Roman Catholic Church at the beginning. Also, Charlemagne attempted to put it back together. Napoleon tried to do so, and also several emperors of Germany. Hitler and Mussolini attempted it, but so far the man has not yet appeared who will accomplish it. God is not quite ready for him to appear.

DESTRUCTION OF GENTILE WORLD POWERS—ESTABLISHMENT OF THE KINGDOM OF HEAVEN UPON EARTH

What will be the final end of this last kingdom, the kingdom of iron mixed with clay? The clay, I believe, represents the masses, the different nations of the ten toes. The iron speaks of the fact that Rome lives on in this final form of the old empire. How is it all going to end? We are given the answer in this concluding section of chapter 2.

> **And in the days of these kings shall the God of heaven set up a kingdom, which shall never be destroyed: and the kingdom shall not be left to other people, but it shall break in pieces and consume all these kingdoms, and it shall stand for ever.**

> **Forasmuch as thou sawest that the stone was cut out of the mountain without hands, and that it brake in pieces the iron, the brass, the clay, the silver, and the gold; the great God hath made known to the king what shall come to pass hereafter: and the dream is certain, and the interpretation thereof sure [Dan. 2:44–45].**

The Antichrist, or the Man of Sin (he has about thirty-five aliases in Scripture), is the one who will bring back the Roman Empire. He will be a world dictator—he will rule the world just as Nebuchadnezzar did at the beginning (see Rev. 13). That is an ideal form of government, but if the wrong man is at the top, it is horrible. This was true of Nebuchadnezzar, as we will see, and it will certainly be true of the Antichrist.

When the Lord Jesus comes, He is going to rule as an autocratic ruler, and He is going to put down all rebellion against Him: "Thou shalt break them with a rod of iron; thou shalt dash them in pieces like a potter's vessel" (Ps. 2:9). I don't think He wants me to apologize for Him today. If you don't like it, I suggest you get on the next trip to the moon or Mars and get off this earth. He is going to take over this earth, and I think He may take over the place you choose, also. This is His universe—it belongs to Him.

"The stone [which] was cut out of the mountain without hands" represents none other than the Lord Jesus Christ. This is not a man; this is God's Anointed. The Lord Jesus Himself made it clear that He is that Stone. In His day there were probably more people who understood what He was saying than there are today. In Matthew 21:44 He said, "And whosoever shall fall on this stone shall be broken: but on whomsoever it shall fall, it will grind him to powder." He is the Stone, the living Stone, the foundation—"For other foundation can no man lay than that is laid, which is Jesus Christ" (1 Cor. 3:11). If you fall on that Stone—that is, rest in Him by faith, come just as you are without one plea but that His blood was shed for you—you are broken, you come as a sinner, with nothing to offer. But He is a wonderful Stone to rest upon.

The Stone is one of many figures of speech in Scripture which speak of Christ in His office as both Savior and Judge. He is the Rock of salvation (see Deut. 32:15), and He is the Rock of judgment (see Deut. 32:4).

These verses in Daniel speak of the time when He is coming to the earth as Judge to put down earth's rebellion against God. The reference here is to the second coming of Christ to the earth, which is depicted for us in detail in Revelation 19:11–21. His coming is going to be climactic, catastrophic, and cataclysmic. It is mentioned again and again in Scripture (see Zech. 14:1–3; Joel 3:2, 9–16; Isa. 34:1–8; Ps. 2).

Man's boast of ruling this earth and establishing a utopia will end in the dismal destruction of this so-called civilization. It is hard for us to get this fact in our thinking: We live in a world that is judged. This world is not on trial. I hear people say, "I'll take my chances." My unsaved friend, you do not have a chance. You are lost. You are without God. You have no capacity for God. All you have in your heart is perhaps a little desire to be religious. You'd like to win a few more ribbons for going to Sunday school—you don't intend to miss a Sunday. But, my friend, you need to trust Christ as Savior, and that is not easy to do, is it? It is not easy to bow to Him and to acknowledge Him. However, either you are going to come to that Stone, or that Stone is coming to you. I'd rather come to the Stone.

God is going to end man's little day down here. God's Kingdom will prevail, and for one thousand years the earth will be tested under the personal reign of Christ. Apart from a brief moment in which Satan and sin will be permitted to make their last assault on the righteous reign of God, the Kingdom will continue on into eternity (see Rev. 20).

> **Then the king Nebuchadnezzar fell upon his face, and worshipped Daniel, and commanded that they should offer an oblation and sweet odours unto him.**
>
> **The king answered unto Daniel, and said, Of a truth it is, that your God is a God of gods, and a Lord of kings, and a revealer of secrets, seeing thou couldest reveal this secret [Dan. 2:46–47].**

The effect of Daniel's interpretation upon Nebuchadnezzar is so profound that he actually worships Daniel and commands others to do likewise. He doesn't know any better; he only knows the worship of physical objects, and he intends thus to worship the living and true God. This was his introduction to the God of heaven. In this book we can watch the growth of faith in the heart of this idolatrous king. It will break through the darkness of paganism, and he is going to come into the marvelous light of the knowledge of God.

> **Then the king made Daniel a great man, and gave him many great gifts, and made him ruler over the whole province of Babylon, and chief of the governors over all the wise men of Babylon.**
>
> **Then Daniel requested of the king, and he set Shadrach, Meshach, and Abed-nego, over the affairs of the province of Babylon: but Daniel sat in the gate of the king [Dan. 2:48–49].**

Sitting in the gate of the king is a practice that is mentioned elsewhere in Scripture. In Genesis, Lot sat in the gate of Sodom; that meant that he was a judge. And in the Book of Esther, Mordecai was also given that office—he sat in the gate as a judge.

Daniel now is rewarded and elevated by Nebuchadnezzar, but he does not forget his three Hebrew friends. They likewise receive high positions in the government of Babylon. This young boy Daniel is moved into a position of sitting in the gate. He was a judge, a Supreme Court Justice, but he also acted in the capacity of prime minister. Throughout this book we will find that he is the one with whom Nebuchadnezzar confers. He judges the people, and he is also prime minister of the kingdom of Babylon.

CHAPTER 3

THEME: The decree of Nebuchadnezzar to enforce universal idolatry; the three Hebrew children cast into the furnace when they refuse to bow to the image of gold

In the first chapter of Daniel heathen customs were judged; in the second chapter heathen philosophy was judged; and in the third chapter heathen pride is judged.

CONSTRUCTION OF THE IMAGE OF GOLD

Nebuchadnezzar the king made an image of gold, whose height was three-score cubits, and the breadth thereof six cubits: he set it up in the plain of Dura, in the province of Babylon.

Then Nebuchadnezzar the king sent to gather together the princes, the governors, and the captains, the judges, the treasurers, the counsellors, the sheriffs, and all the rulers of the provinces, to come to the dedication of the image which Nebuchadnezzar the king had set up [Dan. 3:1–2].

"An image of gold"—this reveals the lavish display of wealth and workmanship which went into the construction of this impressive image.

Some scholars think that Nebuchadnezzar constructed this image in memory of his father, Nabopolassar. Others are equally convinced that he made it to Bel, the pagan god of Babylon. It is more likely that he made it of himself. Daniel had declared that Nebuchadnezzar was the head of gold in the image of his dream. Instead of humbling himself before God, the dream caused Nebuchadnezzar to be filled with excessive pride, and he made an entire image of gold to represent the kingdom he had built.

The image was sixty cubits high and six cubits in breadth—that was a pretty good-sized image. A cubit is approximately eighteen inches, which would make the image ninety feet high. Babylon was situated on a plain, surrounded by flat country. Although it was a city of skyscrapers for its day, the sheer height of the image made it visible for a great distance. The plain of Dura was like an airport—flat and expansive—allowing a great multitude to assemble for the worship of the image, actually the worship of the king.

All the leaders and government officials were present for the dedication of the image. Only the big brass were invited, and they were to sell this project to the people. This was the first step in the brainwashing program. These bureaucrats comprised a great company.

What did Nebuchadnezzar really have in mind in making this image? We can observe here three things: (1) The making of this image shows the rebellion of Nebuchadnezzar against the God of heaven who had given him world dominion. Instead of gratitude, this is a definite act of rebellion. (2) This also shows his vaunted pride in making an image which evidently was self-deification. The Roman emperors also attempted this later on. (3) Obviously, Nebuchadnezzar was seeking a unifying principle to weld together the tribes and tongues and peoples of his kingdom into one great totalitarian government. In other words, he was attempting to institute a world religion. This was nothing in the world but a repetition of the tower of Babel—a forming of one religion for the world.

There are many who are working toward a world religion today, including the denominations which make up the World Council of Churches. They are moving toward a world religion, and, my friend, they are going to leave Jesus out altogether. All of these attempts are not toward the worship of the living and true God; they actually oppose Him. It is a movement which is going to lead to the Great Tribulation period, to the Man of Sin, and the False Prophet. This, of course, is after the true church is removed from the earth (the true church is all those who make up the body of believers). Every believer in

Christ—whoever he is, whatever his color of skin, whatever his denomination, if he is trusting Christ—will go out together.

DEDICATION OF THE IMAGE OF GOLD

**Then the princes, the governors, and captains, the
judges, the treasurers, the counsellors, the sheriffs, and
all the rulers of the provinces, were gathered together
unto the dedication of the image that Nebuchadnezzar
the king had set up; and they stood before the image that
Nebuchadnezzar had set up [Dan. 3:3].**

The day of dedication had arrived. All were present, except Daniel.
We believe he had a good and legitimate reason for his absence. He
probably was away on state business. He was in a unique position of
being the chief advisor to the king of Babylon who was now the ruler
of the world.

The sight of the image of gold on the plain of Dura was very
impressive—as impressive as an Atlas missile set up on the launching
pad at Cape Canaveral, Florida. It must have made a tremendous appeal to the eye.

**Then an herald cried aloud, To you it is commanded, O
people, nations, and languages,**

**That at what time ye hear the sound of the cornet, flute,
harp, sackbut, psaltery, dulcimer, and all kinds of music, ye fall down and worship the golden image that
Nebuchadnezzar the king hath set up:**

**And whoso falleth not down and worshippeth shall the
same hour be cast into the midst of a burning fiery furnace [Dan. 3:4–6].**

They knew nothing of the freedom of worship at this dedication service. When the orchestra began to play, they were to fall down and

worship this image. There was no room here for spontaneous, personal religion—this is all prearranged.

Notice the different instruments in this orchestra: the cornet—that's a wind instrument; the flute—a wind instrument; the harp—a stringed instrument; the sackbut—a trombone, or perhaps a high-stringed instrument; the psaltery—a stringed instrument like the harp; and the dulcimer—a drum with strings above which was played with a stick. Then it says, "and all kinds of music," which means there were instruments and types of music that are not listed.

I would like to give this orchestra a name: the Babylonian Beboppers; or maybe it should be the Babylonian Beatles, or the Royal Rock Quartet Plus Two (or however many instruments there were), or the Chaldean Philharmonic Orchestra.

The point is this: this was more than a dedication—people were forced to worship. However, true worship is an expression of the heart; it cannot be forced. So it is more accurate to say that at least these people went through the outward form of worship.

The music was used to appeal to the flesh. Music that is spiritual is a wonderful aid to worship, but in some of our churches today it is very difficult to tell the difference between spiritual music and worldly music.

Paul had a great deal to say about the importance of music for the believer in worship. He says in Ephesians 5:19, "Speaking to yourselves in psalms and hymns and spiritual songs, singing and making melody in your heart to the Lord." And then in Colossians 3:16 we read: "Let the word of Christ dwell in you richly in all wisdom; teaching and admonishing one another in psalms and hymns and spiritual songs, singing with grace in your hearts to the Lord."

However, at the very beginning, music got off to a bad start. It was mentioned in the godless line of Cain, back in Genesis 4:21—"And his brother's name was Jubal: he was the father of all such as handle the harp and organ."

Whenever music or ritual appeals to the flesh, it degrades man rather than elevates him, and it is not an aid to true worship. It cancels worship out; it deadens everything. However, music can also lift a worship service; it can help the spiritual ministry and be a great blessing.

I recall one particular incident when I was speaking in special meetings held in a fine church in the East. Before my first message, a young lady was called on to sing, and she was quite a showman. Rather than selecting a song which contributed to the worship, she sang a number that simply gave opportunity to show off her voice. When I realized it had deadened the meeting spiritually, I had the congregation sing another hymn before I went on with my message. When I spoke to the pastor about it afterwards, he told me that she was the daughter of one of his leading officers and she always sang at the opening of any special series of meetings!

May I say, music can be helpful to a service or it cannot. Worldly music has a tremendous influence upon people, and it has gotten into many of our churches today. I thank God that many ministers are taking a stand against it.

Nebuchadnezzar had established a terrible penalty for those who refused to worship this image. The music helped prepare for this worldly worship, and you can be sure that everyone in that crowd went down on their faces before the image—with the exception of three young men.

Therefore at that time, when all the people heard the sound of the cornet, flute, harp, sackbut, psaltery, and all kinds of music, all the people, the nations, and the languages, fell down and worshipped the golden image that Nebuchadnezzar the king had set up [Dan. 3:7].

This movement of dedication was an outward act of worship, and practically unanimous. There may have been many who were not convinced in their hearts, but they gave no visible evidence that they were contrary. I am sure they were inwardly attempting to justify their position by some form of rationalization.

We rationalize our own compromises today, also. One man told me that the reason he continued in the liberal church of which he was a member was that his father had been a leader in the church, an outstanding layman, and when he died, the church had dedicated a stained glass window to him. That was the reason he felt he couldn't leave the church! My friend, it would have been better for him to buy a replacement for that window and take the one dedicated to his father with him, than to have continued in that church upon such an unfortunate excuse.

THE THREE HEBREW CHILDREN
FAIL TO WORSHIP THE IMAGE

Wherefore at that time certain Chaldeans came near, and accused the Jews [Dan. 3:8].

The king had apparently appointed observers to note any irregularities in the service. "Certain Chaldeans" may indicate that they had been watching these three Jews particularly, perhaps because they were jealous or had some personal animosity toward them. The only Jews who were involved, of course, were the three Hebrew children who were among the officers of Nebuchadnezzar. The other Jews in captivity who had no position of leadership were not present at this meeting.

They spake and said to the king Nebuchadnezzar, O king, live for ever.

Thou, O king, hast made a decree, that every man that shall hear the sound of the cornet, flute, harp, sackbut, psaltery, and dulcimer, and all kinds of music, shall fall down and worship the golden image:

And whoso falleth not down and worshippeth, that he should be cast into the midst of a burning fiery furnace.

There are certain Jews whom thou hast set over the affairs of the province of Babylon, Shadrach, Meshach, and Abed-nego; these men, O king, have not regarded thee: they serve not thy gods, nor worship the golden image which thou hast set up [Dan. 3:9-12].

This must have been a very famous orchestra in that day—this is the
third time we have been given a list of its instruments.

The Chaldeans' accusation before the king was very formal and
according to protocol. They made a direct charge against the three
Hebrew children by name. There is no misunderstanding as to whom
they referred. Although their insinuation—"These men, O king, have
not regarded thee"—was absolutely false. The Hebrews' refusal to
worship the image was not an act of disloyalty toward the king personally. It was their recognition of a higher power—they were obedient to their God, which will be revealed by their own answer to this
charge.

THE THREE HEBREW CHILDREN DECLARE THE POWER OF GOD

**Then Nebuchadnezzar in his rage and fury commanded
to bring Shadrach, Meshach, and Abed-nego. Then they
brought these men before the king [Dan. 3:13].**

"Nebuchadnezzar in his rage and fury"—this man had a real psychological problem, and such actions characterize his form of insanity. He suffered from hysteria, and a sort of manic-depressive
psychosis: one moment he was hot with anger and the next he was
laughing his head off.

**Nebuchadnezzar spake and said unto them, Is it true, O
Shadrach, Meshach, and Abed-nego, do not ye serve my
gods, nor worship the golden image which I have set
up? [Dan. 3:14].**

Nebuchadnezzar asked them if the charge were true. Had they refused
to worship his gods and the image which he had set up?

**Now if ye be ready that at what time ye hear the sound of
the cornet, flute, harp, sackbut, psaltery, and dulcimer,
and all kinds of music, ye fall down and worship the
image which I have made; well: but if ye worship not, ye**

shall be cast the same hour into the midst of a burning fiery furnace; and who is that God that shall deliver you out of my hands? [Dan. 3:15].

The king gives them another opportunity to change their minds and fall down before the image. Their submission now would be a worse reproach than it would have been at the outset. Nebuchadnezzar again recites the penalty for refusal and shows the fallacy of it. The king has heard of their God before, and he assures them that He is unable to deliver them.

Shadrach, Meshach, and Abed-nego, answered and said to the king, O Nebuchadnezzar, we are not careful to answer thee in this matter [Dan. 3:16].

They address Nebuchadnezzar, but they do not say, "O king, live forever."

"We are not careful to answer thee in this matter" means that they have carefully weighed the consequences of refusing to obey the king. They have counted the cost and are not being "careful" in giving an answer; in other words, they are not being concerned for their own well-being in the answer they give to the king.

The wise men in Babylon would have advised the Hebrews to fall down and worship, but God had said: "Thou shalt have no other gods before me. Thou shalt not make unto thee any graven image, or any likeness of any thing that is in heaven above, or that is in the earth beneath, or that is in the water under the earth: Thou shalt not bow down thyself to them, nor serve them: for I the LORD thy God am a jealous God, visiting the iniquity of the fathers upon the children unto the third and fourth generation of them that hate me; And shewing mercy unto thousands of them that love me, and keep my commandments" (Exod. 20:3-6). These Hebrew children were being true to God, and it took a great deal of courage for them to take this position.

If it be so, our God whom we serve is able to deliver us from the burning fiery furnace, and he will deliver us out of thine hand, O king.

**But if not, be it known unto thee, O king, that we will
not serve thy gods, nor worship the golden image which
thou hast set up [Dan. 3:17-18].**

They make it very clear: "If it is God's will, He will deliver us out of
your hand." Regardless of the outcome, these three had purposed to
serve God and not the idol of Nebuchadnezzar.

THE THREE HEBREWS ARE PRESERVED
IN THE FIERY FURNACE

**Then was Nebuchadnezzar full of fury, and the form of
his visage was changed against Shadrach, Meshach,
and Abed-nego: therefore he spake, and commanded
that they should heat the furnace one seven times more
than it was wont to be heated.**

**And he commanded the most mighty men that were in
his army to bind Shadrach, Meshach, and Abed-nego,
and to cast them into the burning fiery furnace [Dan.
3:19-20].**

"Full of fury"—Nebuchadnezzar had an uncontrollable temper. In
an extreme outrage of emotionalism, Nebuchadnezzar vented his anger against these men whom he had previously favored. The fire in the
furnace was to be built up *seven times* larger and hotter than usual!
This was not necessary, but it reveals what was in this man's heart.

**Then these men were bound in their coats, their hosen,
and their hats, and their other garments, and were cast
into the midst of the burning fiery furnace [Dan. 3:21].**

"Their hosen" means their stockings. In other words, they were in full
dress for this trip to the fiery furnace.

**Therefore because the king's commandment was ur-
gent, and the furnace exceeding hot, the flame of the fire**

slew those men that took up Shadrach, Meshach, and
Abed-nego.

And these three men, Shadrach, Meshach, and Abed-
nego, fell down bound into the midst of the burning fiery
furnace [Dan. 3:22–23].

The haste and high temperature caused those who threw in the captives to perish in the flames.

Then Nebuchadnezzar the king was astonied, and rose
up in haste, and spake, and said unto his counsellors,
Did not we cast three men bound into the midst of the
fire? They answered and said unto the king, True, O
king.

He answered and said, Lo, I see four men loose, walking in the midst of the fire, and they have no hurt; and
the form of the fourth is like the Son of God [Dan.
3:24–25].

This furnace apparently was an open furnace, and Nebuchadnezzar,
who expected these men to expire at once, was amazed to see them
alive and walking about in the fire.

Another amazing fact was to see a fourth Man whom Nebuchadnezzar described as being in the form "like the Son of God." That
should be translated "like a son of gods." Nebuchadnezzar had no
knowledge of the living and true God at this time, although Daniel
had spoken of Him. Having no spiritual perception, Nebuchadnezzar
could only testify to His unusual appearance—He looked like one of
the sons of the gods. However, I do believe that the fourth Man was the
Son of God, the preincarnate Christ.

The preservation of these faithful few in the fiery furnace was miraculous. There is no other explanation—you either accept that or reject it. Either the Book of Daniel is misrepresenting things, or it is
telling the truth. We have a group today, often identified as neo-
orthodox, who rob the language of Scripture of its true meaning. They

castrate the meaning of the language, saying it doesn't mean what it says, but that it means something "spiritual." That type of rationalism is not only hypocritical, it is deceptive.

Several years ago a retired pastor told me of his visit to an outstanding church in Southern California where the son of a friend of his was the pastor. He told me that in his sermon the young man used language that he was accustomed to hearing in the pulpit, and he went up afterwards and congratulated him. "Why, you used in your message the same language John Wesley used!" The young man responded to this retired preacher, "I used the same language John Wesley used, but I do not mean what John Wesley meant by it." That was positively deceptive—taking language and trying to explain away its real meaning.

My point is that there are many miracles in Scripture that such men have attempted to explain away. For instance, Jesus didn't walk on the water—He walked on the shore, and the disciples *thought* He was walking on the water. The widow's son was not really dead—they only *thought* he was—and Jesus just woke him up. That type of double-talk is deceptive and hypocritical. You either believe this miracle or you don't. No three men can be thrown into a fiery furnace without being absolutely destroyed, unless a miracle takes place. I believe a miracle took place, and that the fourth Man present was none other than the Lord Jesus Christ.

The events recorded here in this chapter are a historical incident, but we should also note that it is an adumbration, a prophetic picture, of the Great Tribulation period. The fiery furnace represents the suffering that will occur during the Great Tribulation. This man Nebuchadnezzar represents the beast out of the sea, the Antichrist, the last great world ruler. This image of gold represents the abomination of desolation of which the Lord Jesus spoke. These three Hebrew children represent the remnant which will be miraculously preserved during the Great Tribulation period. And then, quite interestingly, Daniel is not mentioned in this chapter at all. He wasn't around. Apparently he acted not only as a Supreme Court Justice, but also as prime minister of the kingdom. He was out on kingdom business, out on the king's highway somewhere. He is therefore, a picture of the redeemed ones who are to be removed before the Great Tribulation. What a very wonderful picture is presented here!

In the fourth Man present in the furnace, we see that the Lord Jesus was there with them. He will be with them also in the day of the Great Tribulation, with those who are His as they go through the trials of that period. My friend, He is with you and me today as we go through our trials. He said, "These things I have spoken unto you, that in me ye might have peace. In the world ye shall have tribulation: but be of good cheer; I have overcome the world" (John 16:33). He also said, ". . . lo, I am with you alway, even unto the end of the world" (Matt. 28:20). He promises never to leave or forsake His own.

> **Then Nebuchadnezzar came near to the mouth of the burning fiery furnace, and spake, and said, Shadrach, Meshach, and Abed-nego, ye servants of the most high God, come forth, and come hither. Then Shadrach, Meshach, and Abed-nego, came forth of the midst of the fire.**

> **And the princes, governors, and captains, and the king's counsellors, being gathered together, saw these men, upon whose bodies the fire had no power, nor was an hair of their head singed, neither were their coats changed, nor the smell of fire had passed on them [Dan. 3:26–27].**

Nebuchadnezzar acknowledges that these three are "servants of the most high God." I think he is getting a little closer to a knowledge of God. These men came forth with not a hair singed, nor the smell of smoke on their garments! This is a clear-cut miracle.

NEBUCHADNEZZAR'S DECREE CONCERNING THE GOD OF THE HEBREW CHILDREN

> **Then Nebuchadnezzar spake, and said, Blessed be the God of Shadrach, Meshach, and Abed-nego, who hath**

sent his angel, and delivered his servants that trusted in him, and have changed the king's word, and yielded their bodies, that they might not serve nor worship any god, except their own God.

Therefore I make a decree, That every people, nation, and language, which speak any thing amiss against the God of Shadrach, Meshach, and Abed-nego, shall be cut in pieces, and their houses shall be made a dunghill: because there is no other God that can deliver after this sort.

Then the king promoted Shadrach, Meshach, and Abed-nego, in the province of Babylon [Dan. 3:28–30].

There is nothing personal in this expression of Nebuchadnezzar; yet he recognizes the omnipotence of the living God and His power in delivering these three men. He grants that their God is superior to his. This is Nebuchadnezzar's conviction; in the next chapter, we will read his personal testimony of conversion. I believe he came to the knowledge of the living and true God. It took this man a long time to move out of the paganism and heathenism in which he was saturated.

Now these three Hebrew children are back in Nebuchadnezzar's favor. Twice they had the sentence of death upon them, twice they have been miraculously delivered, and twice they have been promoted.

In the same way the Lord Jesus is able to keep His own in the world today. That ought to be a comforting thought to many of us. He said in John 10:27–28: "My sheep hear my voice, and I know them, and they follow me: And I give unto them eternal life; and they shall never perish, neither shall any man pluck them out of my hand." And again in John 17:11—"And now I am no more in the world, but these are in the world, and I come to thee. Holy Father, keep through thine own name those whom thou hast given me, that they may be one, as we are." He continued, "I pray not that thou shouldest take them out of the world, but that thou shouldest keep them from the evil [one]"

(John 17:15). In Hebrews 7:25 we read: "Wherefore he is able also to save them to the uttermost that come unto God by him, seeing he ever liveth to make intercession for them." And finally, Paul wrote, "For the which cause I also suffer these things: nevertheless I am not ashamed: for I know whom I have believed, and am persuaded that he is able to keep that which I have committed unto him against that day" (2 Tim. 1:12).

My friend, you and I are living in a world today in which we are going to have trouble. Some of God's children do get into a fiery furnace, but He is able to keep them even there, and He is able to bring them out of it. We simply do not trust the Lord like we should—we do not have the faith of these three Hebrew children.

CHAPTER 4

THEME: Testimony of Nebuchadnezzar; tree dream of Nebuchadnezzar; tree dream interpreted by Daniel; the mental malady of Nebuchadnezzar; dream fulfilled and Nebuchadnezzar's reason restored

This chapter is going to give us a great deal more information about this man Nebuchadnezzar than we have had before. Actually, there was a skeleton in the family closet—something I am sure they didn't boast of: Nebuchadnezzar suffered from a form of insanity. This chapter is a leaf of history taken from the archives of Babylon. Nebuchadnezzar's form of insanity is pretty well identified and known today, and it is something which a number of world rulers have suffered from.

We are living in a day when a great deal of attention is given to mental illness and various forms of abnormal behavior. I wonder sometimes just who is normal in this mad world in which we live! A psychologist will tell you that the bulk of mankind is normal, a few are abnormal, and a few are above normal or geniuses. Who is to say who is sane and who is not sane? The standard, of course, is the way most of us act—the behavior of the majority is called normal. When just a few react, that is abnormal, which, of course, is an arbitrary distinction. Who in the world is going to say that what the majority is doing today is normal? That could be quite a subject of debate, and I think it would be very difficult to sustain a thesis that the majority of us are normal. In Shakespeare's play *Hamlet*, Hamlet was sent from Denmark over to England (they thought he was a little touched in the head) because, they said, in England everyone was abnormal!

There is the story of the man who had trouble sleeping at night because he had the feeling that there was someone under his bed. He was losing sleep because he had to get up many times during the night to look under the bed and satisfy himself that no one was there. He finally went to the psychiatrist with his problem. The psychiatrist told him, "Well, you really do have a problem, and it is going to be difficult to bring you back to normal, but I think we can do it. It will take ten sessions, and it will cost you twenty-five dollars for each session." The man left, saying he would think it over and let him know. However, he never returned. Several weeks later the psychiatrist met the man on the street and asked him why he had never come back. The man replied that he had been cured with the help of a carpenter friend of his. He had told his friend his problem, and the carpenter said he could fix it for him. He came over to the man's house with his saw and simply sawed off the legs of the bed. "Now that fellow *can't* get under my bed!" the man told the psychiatrist. I guess a lot of us suffer some kind of abnormality, but this man Nebuchadnezzar had a real problem.

TESTIMONY OF NEBUCHADNEZZAR

Nebuchadnezzar the king, unto all people, nations, and languages, that dwell in all the earth; Peace be multiplied unto you.

I thought it good to shew the signs and wonders that the high God hath wrought toward me.

How great are his signs! and how mighty are his wonders! his kingdom is an everlasting kingdom, and his dominion is from generation to generation [Dan. 4:1–3].

This is Nebuchadnezzar's marvelous testimony, and it shows development in the faith of this man. Back in Daniel 3:29 he issued a decree and expressed a conviction. Here he gives a personal testimony. There it was a decree; here it is a decision. There it was a conviction, and here it is conversion. Chronologically, this testimony should come at the end of this chapter because it grew out of his experience recorded here.

Nebuchadnezzar sends a message of peace to "all peoples, nations, and languages" of his kingdom. He is not speaking of peace among nations—he already has such peace, attained by his military might and enforced by his superior power. Rather, he speaks here of the peace of heart which comes to a sinner when he knows he has been accepted of God and is at peace with God. This man's own tranquility was restored to him, as we shall see in this chapter.

He speaks also of what "the high God hath wrought toward me." His testimony is very personal. God is no longer the God of only the three Hebrew children. He also testifies to God's signs, His wonders, and His dominion. He recognizes and acknowledges that God's rule, God's kingdom, is above his.

The peace of which Nebuchadnezzar speaks can only come to the human heart when it knows God. "Therefore being justified by faith, we have peace with God through our Lord Jesus Christ" (Rom. 5:1)— that is the peace which He made by the blood of the Cross. It is the peace which can come to a sinner's heart that is all right now because of the penalty which Christ paid—God is for him now and God is on his side. Back of all the trouble and travail that is in the world today, back of all the troubled hearts, is the question of sin. Things are not right. One young fellow expressed it this way to me: "I'm not at peace with myself. I'm not at peace with my parents. I'm not at peace with my teachers. I'm not at peace with anybody." Fundamentally, man must make peace with God. When there is peace in the human heart, then there can be peace made with those round about us; but, until then, man does not know peace.

I am sure that much of what is called abnormality and insanity today could be cured by bringing the gospel and the knowledge of God to the people who are so afflicted. I thought it was absurd that hospitals were set up to receive the Vietnam War POW's as they arrived in the Philippine Islands. They were to be examined and given psychological tests there. However, the men came bounding off the planes, ready to make phone calls to a wife, a mother, or some other loved one. Many of them testified that God had been with them. They had learned to pray, and Christ had been with them. They didn't need a lot of psychological treatment.

Everything in the world is being taught in our schools and colleges except the Word of God. It is the Word of God which can bring peace to the human heart. This is the problem Nebuchadnezzar had, but he made his peace with God, and God made peace with him. Today, God has already made peace with you—He is waiting for you to make peace with Him. When you have settled that, you won't need to spend much time on the psychiatrist's couch. Instead, you will be a radiant Christian.

TREE DREAM OF NEBUCHADNEZZAR

We find the first symptom of Nebuchadnezzar's form of insanity in verse 4—

> I Nebuchadnezzar was at rest in mine house, and flourishing in my palace [Dan. 4:4].

The personal pronouns—my, I, and mine—are already used three times in just this one verse. You will find them about three times in every verse from verse 4 through verse 10. Nebuchadnezzar had a bad case of what I call "perpendicular I-itis." Job had that problem also.

> I saw a dream which made me afraid, and the thoughts upon my bed and the visions of my head troubled me [Dan. 4:5].

It is all about me and mine.

> Therefore made I a decree to bring in all the wise men of Babylon before me, that they might make known unto me the interpretation of the dream.

> Then came in the magicians, the astrologers, the Chaldeans, and the soothsayers: and I told the dream before them; but they did not make known unto me the interpretation thereof.

> But at the last Daniel came in before me, whose name was Belteshazzar, according to the name of my god, and in whom is the spirit of the holy gods: and before him I told the dream, saying,

O Belteshazzar, master of the magicians, because I know that the spirit of the holy gods is in thee, and no secret troubleth thee, tell me the visions of my dream that I have seen, and the interpretation thereof [Dan. 4:6–9].

Again the wise men were called in and were unable to give an interpretation of the dream. It was God who gave both of his dreams, and only God could give the interpretation. Finally, Daniel was called in. Nebuchadnezzar had learned that Daniel was a Spirit-filled man and that interpretations were given him by God.

Nebuchadnezzar is introducing the vision that he has had, and he gives us a surplus of the personal pronoun *I*.

I think that the family had kept this man's insanity quiet. They didn't talk much about it, but those closest to him did recognize it. I believe the psychiatrists today would label it hysteria. Hysteria is a highly emotional mental disease. It is psychotic, rather than a structural form of insanity (in other words, Nebuchadnezzar was not insane because he had been dropped on his head as a baby). It manifests itself in somnambulism (sleepwalking) and amnesia (loss of memory), and it is thought to be hereditary. A historian tells us that a number of other world rulers have suffered from some form of mental instability: Antiochus Epiphanes, Charles VI of France, Christian VII of Denmark, George III of England, Otho of Bavaria, Alexander the Great, Julius Caesar and Napoleon. It has also been in the Spanish royal line, the Russian line (among the czars), and also in the English line. Henry VI of England was a real madhatter, and suffered from something similar to hysteria. Hitler also had that problem. And here, the head of gold, Nebuchadnezzar, was a lunatic. He had bats in his belfry. He was not ruling with a full deck in his hands. He was just a little off, if you please. All of this was revealed in his extreme emotionalism—he would move in any direction and to an extreme.

The whole key to this chapter is found in verse 17, and it is important to note it at this point: "This matter is by the decree of the watchers, and the demand by the word of the holy ones: to the intent that the living may know that the most High ruleth in the kingdom of men, and giveth it to whomsoever he will, and setteth up over it the basest of men." God says that He puts on the thrones of this world the basest of men. In other words, God gives us the kind of rulers we deserve and the kind we want. There have been many rulers who had bats in their belfries and who were off their rockers. God says He sets over the kingdoms the basest of men: twenty-five hundred years of history since Nebuchadnezzar have demonstrated the truth of this statement.

Thus were the visions of mine head in my bed; I saw, and behold, a tree in the midst of the earth, and the height thereof was great.

The tree grew, and was strong, and the height thereof reached unto heaven, and the sight thereof to the end of all the earth:

The leaves thereof were fair, and the fruit thereof much, and in it was meat for all: the beasts of the field had shadow under it, and the fowls of the heaven dwelt in the boughs thereof, and all flesh was fed of it.

I saw in the visions of my head upon my bed, and, behold, a watcher and an holy one came down from heaven;

He cried aloud, and said thus, Hew down the tree, and cut off his branches, shake off his leaves, and scatter his fruit: let the beasts get away from under it, and the fowls from his branches:

Nevertheless leave the stump of his roots in the earth, even with a band of iron and brass, in the tender grass of the field; and let it be wet with the dew of heaven, and let his portion be with the beasts in the grass of the earth:

Let his heart be changed from man's, and let a beast's heart be given unto him; and let seven times pass over him [Dan. 4:10–16].

These verses contain the substance of Nebuchadnezzar's dream which centers around a tree that grew tall to heaven, wide enough to fill the earth. The tree was evidently an evergreen, for its leaves were fair. It was a fruit tree, and its fruit was eaten by all. Beasts stood in its shadow, and birds rested in its branches.

In Scripture, a tree can represent a number of things. A tree can represent a man: "And he shall be like a tree planted by the rivers of water, that bringeth forth his fruit in his season; his leaf also shall not wither; and whatsoever he doeth shall prosper" (Ps. 1:3; see also Jer. 17:8; Isa. 56:3). Also a tree can represent a nation (see Ezek. 31:3–14; Matt. 24:32–33). The mustard tree in Matthew 13:31 and 32 represents Christendom today. The olive tree represents both Israel and the Gentiles (see Rom. 11:16–24). The tree here represents Nebuchadnezzar primarily and also his kingdom of Babylon—the king and kingdom are inseparable.

The "watcher" and "holy one" are of an order of God's created intelligences. The watchers are the holy ones who administer the affairs of this world. The Book of Daniel makes it very clear that God has created intelligences who administer His universe and this world in which you and I live. God has His administrators under which are many created intelligences. Over against that, Satan also has his minions who have charge over certain areas of certain nations. We will see more of this in the Book of Daniel.

These watchers see all, hear all, and tell all. Many believers today think they can live in secret, that they are not under the eye of God. We talk about wanting to enjoy our privacy, but if you want to know the truth, you and I haven't any privacy. Psalm 139:7–12 tells us that we cannot get away from God, no matter where we go. Secret sin on earth is open scandal up yonder in heaven. His created intelligences know all about you, and if you are a Christian, you had better go to God with that "secret" sin in your life and get it straightened out.

Now the tree was hewn down, and a band of iron and brass was put around its stump to indicate that it would grow and flourish again in seven years. And the heart of the ruler (that is, of the "tree") was to be changed into that of a beast—the vegetable was to become an animal.

This matter is by the decree of the watchers, and the demand by the word of the holy ones: to the intent that the living may know that the most High ruleth in the kingdom of men, and giveth it to whomsoever he will, and setteth up over it the basest of men [Dan. 4:17].

There are three things that we learn from Nebuchadnezzar's dream:

1. "The most High ruleth in the kingdom of men." If you think that God has abdicated today and has withdrawn from this universe, you are wrong. The universe has not gotten loose from Him. Emerson was wrong when he said, "Things are in the saddle, and they ride mankind." There happens to be Somebody else in the saddle, and He is in control on this earth. "He that sitteth in the heavens shall laugh: the Lord shall have them in derision. Then shall he speak unto them in his wrath, and vex them in his sore displeasure. Yet have I set my king upon my holy hill of Zion" (Ps. 2:4–6). God says He is going on with His purpose in the world. He is permitting Satan to carry out a nefarious plot for a very definite reason: God is demonstrating something to His created intelligences today. There are a lot of silly things being said about Satan which are entirely unscriptural.

Nations rise and fall to teach men that God rules and overrules the kingdoms of this world. If you think our nation happens to be His special little pet, you are entirely wrong. I believe we have already been put on the auction block: we are already judged. The downward course which this nation is traveling is going to take us right to the judgment of God. He rules in the kingdom of men.

2. He "giveth it to whomsoever he will." You probably thought that the Democrats and the Republicans put men in power. They think they do, but God disposes of these kingdoms according to His will. That thought may cause someone's chest to puff up, and he will say, "Well, I am occupying this office by the will of God." A lot of kings in the past had the foolish notion that they were ruling in God's place. Don't believe a word of it—God puts them in power. Notice that Paul says in Romans 13:1, ". . . the powers that be are ordained of God." Why in the world does God permit certain powers to rule on this earth?

3. He "setteth up over it the basest of men." This third statement should be humbling to both the Democrats and the Republicans—and to all of mankind. If you think we pick the best men, we don't—all you need to do is to read human history to see this. My study of English history shows that our ancestors in the British Isles were some pretty bloody ancestors. They were terrible, and they had some rulers who were unspeakable! May I say to you, God "setteth up over it the basest of men," and we get the kind of ruler that we deserve. People complain about our government, our Congress, and all that sort of thing. My friend, we put them in their offices; we voted for them. God lets the basest of men come to power. That ought to be humbling to all of us—from Washington, D.C., on down. You will never hear of someone who is trying to curry the favor of our leaders speaking on this verse at a Presidential breakfast or upon any occasion in Washington! This verse is quite upsetting, is it not?

History will substantiate the truth of this statement. The head of gold, Nebuchadnezzar, was insane; yet he was a brilliant ruler who formed the first world kingdom. He had times when he was as mad as a mad-hatter and didn't even know who he was. As we have mentioned before, many of the great world rulers have suffered problems similar to his. And the reason our forefathers did not establish the United States of America as a kingdom is because they believed that no man could be trusted to rule. God has been demonstrating this now over quite a length of time: He "setteth up over it the basest of men."

> **This dream I king Nebuchadnezzar have seen. Now thou, O Belteshazzar, declare the interpretation thereof, forasmuch as all the wise men of my kingdom are not able to make known unto me the interpretation: but thou art able; for the spirit of the holy gods is in thee [Dan. 4:18].**

Now Daniel will interpret Nebuchadnezzar's dream.

TREE DREAM INTERPRETED BY DANIEL

**Then Daniel, whose name was Belteshazzar, was aston-
ished for one hour, and his thoughts troubled him. The
king spake, and said, Belteshazzar, let not the dream,
or the interpretation thereof, trouble thee. Belteshazzar
answered and said, My lord, the dream be to them that
hate thee, and the interpretation thereof to thine enemies [Dan. 4:19].**

The dream is a great shock and a blow to Daniel. Nebuchadnezzar has
become his friend, and Daniel is his prime minister. The first dream
Nebuchadnezzar had dignified him, but this dream debases him. It is
so bad that Daniel is reluctant to reveal it to the king.

Daniel resists whatever temptation there may have been to with-
hold from Nebuchadnezzar the full story. He is going to give the entire
interpretation to the king. The question is often raised as to whether a
doctor should tell his patient that he is suffering from a fatal disease. I
personally feel that if a man is getting ready to take the biggest step of
his life, he ought to know it—that is, if there is someone else who
knows it. I have always appreciated the fact that my doctor, who is a
Christian and a cancer specialist, said to me when he discovered that I
had cancer: "Dr. McGee, I'm going to tell you exactly what the situation is, because if I didn't, you would never trust me." I appreciated
that. Many people would simply want their doctor to butter them up
and assure them they are well.

Daniel is going to lay it on the line to Nebuchadnezzar, and he uses
a great deal of tact in approaching the problem. First, he tells Nebuchadnezzar that the good in the dream is for the enemies of the king.

**The tree that thou sawest, which grew, and was strong,
whose height reached unto the heaven, and the sight
thereof to all the earth;**

**Whose leaves were fair, and the fruit thereof much, and
in it was meat for all; under which the beasts of the field**

dwelt, and upon whose branches the fowls of the heaven
had their habitation:

It is thou, O king, that art grown and become strong: for
thy greatness is grown, and reacheth unto heaven, and
thy dominion to the end of the earth [Dan. 4:20–22].

The tree represents Nebuchadnezzar. He has grown strong and become great. He is a world ruler and has filled the then-civilized world.
The picture here is of Nebuchadnezzar personally and of his dominion.

And whereas the king saw a watcher and an holy one
coming down from heaven, and saying, Hew the tree
down, and destroy it; yet leave the stump of the roots
thereof in the earth, even with a band of iron and brass,
in the tender grass of the field; and let it be wet with the
dew of heaven, and let his portion be with the beasts of
the field, till seven times pass over him;

This is the interpretation, O king, and this is the decree
of the most High, which is come upon my lord the king
[Dan. 4:23–24].

The tree (Nebuchadnezzar) is to be cut off but not totally rejected. For
seven years, Nebuchadnezzar is to live with and like the beasts of the
field. He won't even recognize who he is.

That they shall drive thee from men, and thy dwelling
shall be with the beasts of the field, and they shall make
thee to eat grass as oxen, and they shall wet thee with
the dew of heaven, and seven times shall pass over thee,
till thou know that the most High ruleth in the kingdom
of men, and giveth it to whomsoever he will.

And whereas they commanded to leave the stump of the
tree roots; thy kingdom shall be sure unto thee, after
that thou shalt have known that the heavens do rule
[Dan. 4:25–26].

Daniel makes it clear why this dream was given to Nebuchadnezzar and why he is going to have this experience. Nebuchadnezzar is lifted up with pride, which was evidenced when he made that tremendous image and forced all mankind to fall down and worship him. This man is certainly filled with pride, and now God is going to humble him. He is to be driven out of his palace, out to the pasture where he will take his abode with the oxen and forget what manner of man he was. However, God is also going to bring Nebuchadnezzar out of his insanity.

Evidently Nebuchadnezzar suffered from hysteria; some of the symptoms which are evident in his life are characteristic of this form of abnormality. One of the symptoms is excessive emotionalism, actually a sort of manic-depressive psychosis. One moment the patient is joyful and friendly, and the next he is morose and antagonistic. Someone has expressed it as "Easy gloom, easy glow"—it is an up and down state. Many people suffer from it to some extent. We all know people who are moody at times and then very joyful at others. But this was a very real problem for Nebuchadnezzar. It was a functional problem and not a structural one; it was not the result of some injury to his brain.

Nebuchadnezzar's hysteria also manifested itself in amnesia. Those afflicted with this malady don't know who they are for a period of time. There are those in mental institutions, for example, who think they are Napoleon or some such person. Nebuchadnezzar thought he was an animal.

Another thing that identifies hysteria is extreme egotism and pride. This became an obsession with Nebuchadnezzar (see Dan. 4:30). We saw how in verses 4 through 10, he talked about I, I, I—he had a bad case of perpendicular I-itis.

Pride is one of the things God hates, and it is something that characterizes man. Old Caesar Augustus said of a city which he captured, "I found it brick, I left it straw." He had utterly destroyed it. Another caesar made the statement "I found Rome wood, and I left it marble." You see, pride is the besetting sin of the human family. But what does man have to be proud of? Jeremiah 9:23–24 says, "Thus saith the LORD, Let not the wise man glory in his wisdom, neither let the mighty man glory in his might, let not the rich man glory in his riches: But let him that glorieth glory in this, that he understandeth and knoweth me, that I am the LORD which exercise lovingkindness, judgment, and righteousness, in the earth: for in these things I delight, saith the LORD."

God's salvation rules out pride—that is one thing you cannot have when you come to Christ for salvation. Paul said, "For I determined not to know any thing among you, save Jesus Christ, and him crucified" (1 Cor. 2:2). We have nothing in which we can glory. Again, the apostle wrote, "For who maketh thee to differ from another? and what hast thou that thou didst not receive? now if thou didst receive it, why dost thou glory, as if thou hadst not received it?" (1 Cor. 4:7). And finally, in 2 Corinthians 10:17, we read: "But he that glorieth, let him glory in the Lord." Pride is number one on God's "hate parade"—He hates pride (see Prov. 6:16–19). Our Lord Jesus gave us the ultimate example of humility: "And being found in fashion as a man, he humbled himself, and became obedient unto death, even the death of the cross" (Phil. 2:8).

Finally, it is characteristic of hysteria that it runs in cycles. In Nebuchadnezzar's case, it was a cycle of seven years.

Wherefore, O king, let my counsel be acceptable unto thee, and break off thy sins by righteousness, and thine iniquities by shewing mercy to the poor; if it may be a lengthening of thy tranquility [Dan. 4:27].

This man Nebuchadnezzar is disturbed within his own heart—he has no peace. He has brought peace to the world—there is no one to challenge his authority at this time—but he is living in sin. Daniel tells Nebuchadnezzar that he needs to repent of and turn from his sins. He needs to turn to God and to a life of righteousness. Daniel advises him to repent in order to reverse the coming judgment. There is still hope for deliverance—Nebuchadnezzar could know the peace and tranquility of God. I think this is God's final warning to Nebuchadnezzar.

A great deal of the mental and emotional abnormalities that we see today are actually the result of spiritual problems. Now I do not say that they all are, as I know that there is sometimes a structural basis for such a problem. However, much of the disturbed condition we see in the lives of men is rooted in the the spiritual condition of men. There is peace for them, if they would only come to Christ.

THE MENTAL MALADY OF NEBUCHADNEZZAR

All this came upon the king Nebuchadnezzar.

At the end of twelve months he walked in the palace of the kingdom of Babylon.

The king spake, and said, Is not this great Babylon, that I have built for the house of the kingdom by the might of my power, and for the honour of my majesty? [Dan. 4:28-30].

Nebuchadnezzar did not heed the warning of Daniel. One year of grace went by before judgment fell. How patient God is! But His graciousness and longsuffering are not understood by the wicked (see Eccl. 8:11).

The king was on the verge of a mental break. He looked about his great kingdom, the kingdom which God had already told him that He had given to him. Despite that, Nebuchadnezzar now says, "Is not this great Babylon, that I have built?"

There have been a multitude of men and women throughout history who have tried to build little empires, and they have looked upon them with pride. I sometimes have opportunity to advise young preachers, and I tell them, "Look fellows, don't try to build a little empire of your church. I started out with that viewpoint, and I'll be honest with you, I have never been more disturbed or unhappy as I was then." This passage of Scripture in Daniel really spoke to me one day, and I realized I was trying to be an empire builder—and that wasn't what God intended for me to be. My ministry is building the lives of people, not trying to build a great empire. So I tell young preachers, "Start building in the lives of people, and I think the Lord will let you have what He wants you to have."

While the word was in the king's mouth, there fell a voice from heaven, saying, O king Nebuchadnezzar, to thee it is spoken; The kingdom is departed from thee.

And they shall drive thee from men, and thy dwelling shall be with the beasts of the field: they shall make thee to eat grass as oxen, and seven times shall pass over thee, until thou know that the most High ruleth in the kingdom of men, and giveth it to whomsoever he will.

The same hour was the thing fulfilled upon Nebuchadnezzar: and he was driven from men, and did eat grass as oxen, and his body was wet with the dew of heaven, till his hairs were grown like eagles' feathers, and his nails like birds' claws [Dan. 4:31–33].

Nebuchadnezzar moves out of the palace, out yonder to live with nature. God deals with this man personally. As he departs from the plane of normality and rationality, his kingdom slips from him. The insane of that day were driven out rather than being placed in an institution for treatment. Under ordinary circumstances Nebuchadnezzar would never have been able to return to the throne; yet God promised that he would do so after he had learned his lesson.

History corroborates this event in the life of Nebuchadnezzar. Dr. Philip R. Newell has this note from Albert Barnes, "Josephus attributes to the Babylonian historian, Berosus, a definite reference concerning a strange malady suffered by Nebuchadnezzar before his death" (Daniel, the Man Greatly Beloved, and His Prophecies, p. 54).

DREAM FULFILLED AND NEBUCHADNEZZAR'S REASON RESTORED

And at the end of the days I Nebuchadnezzar lifted up mine eyes unto heaven, and mine understanding returned unto me, and I blessed the most High, and I praised and honoured him that liveth for ever, whose

> dominion is an everlasting dominion, and his kingdom
> is from generation to generation [Dan. 4:34].

His understanding comes back to him, and he adds these brief words to the testimony which he gave at the opening of this chapter.

> And all the inhabitants of the earth are reputed as noth-
> ing: and he doeth according to his will in the army of
> heaven, and among the inhabitants of the earth: and
> none can stay his hand, or say unto him, What doest
> thou? [Dan. 4:35].

Nebuchadnezzar has learned now that God is running things, that He is in control of this universe. Nebuchadnezzar accepted this thing that had come to him as the will of God for him, yielding his proud mind to the will of God. That is what a great many believers need to do today.

> At the same time my reason returned unto me; and for
> the glory of my kingdom, mine honour and brightness
> returned unto me; and my counsellors and my lords
> sought unto me; and I was established in my kingdom,
> and excellent majesty was added unto me.

> Now I Nebuchadnezzar praise and extol and honour the
> King of heaven, all whose works are truth, and his ways
> judgment: and those that walk in pride he is able to
> abase [Dan. 4:36–37].

Nebuchadnezzar's reason returned to him. His position as king of Babylon was restored to him, and his officials once again surrounded him. The kingdom was not jeopardized during his long period of absence, and added majesty came to him because he had now come to the knowledge of the living and true God.

CHAPTER 5

THEME: Feast of Belshazzar; fingers of God write upon the wall; failure of the wise men to read the handwriting; Daniel spurns the king's gifts; Daniel interprets the handwriting on the wall; fall of Babylon— fulfillment that very night

The events recorded in chapter 5 took place a great deal later than those in the previous chapters. Again, this is just a page lifted from the historical records of Babylon, and much has taken place since the events of chapter 4.

FEAST OF BELSHAZZAR

Belshazzar the king made a great feast to a thousand of his lords, and drank wine before the thousand [Dan. 5:1].

Now who was Belshazzar and how did he get to the throne? In the previous chapter the king was Nebuchadnezzar. Belshazzar has been a controversial figure in history, so we do need to take a moment to look at him. Even Dean Farrar said, "There was no such king as Belshazzar." John Walvoord in his book *Daniel, the Key to Prophetic Revelation*, p. 114, states: "Until the discovery of the Nabonidus Cylinder, no mention of Belshazzar, whom Daniel declares to be king of Babylon, had been found in extrabiblical literature. Critics of the authenticity and historicity of Daniel accordingly were free to question whether any such person as Belshazzar existed. Since the publication of Raymond Dougherty's scholarly research on Nabonidus and Belshazzar, based on the Nabonidus Cylinder and other sources, there is no ground for questioning the general historicity of Belshazzar . . . ." The name of Bel-shar-usur (Belshazzar) has been found on cylinders in which he is called the son of Nabonidus. It is now generally accepted that Belshazzar acted as a regent under his father, Nabonidus.

A résumé of the events which succeeded Nebuchadnezzar's reign would be helpful at this point. At the death of Nebuchadnezzar his only son, Evil-merodach, succeeded him, in about 561 B.C. (see 2 Kings 25:27). Evil-merodach was murdered by Nergal-sharezer who had married one of Nebuchadnezzar's daughters and now replaced him on the throne in about 559 B.C. Nergal-sharezer was succeeded by his young son who reigned only a few months before he was murdered by Nabonidus (the husband of another of Nebuchadnezzar's daughters). Nabonidus, the last ruler of the Babylonian empire, spent much of his time away from the kingdom on foreign expeditions, and Belshazzar his son remained at Babylon as his co-regent. All this reveals the accuracy of what Jeremiah the prophet had said: "And now have I given all these lands into the hand of Nebuchadnezzar the king of Babylon, my servant; and the beasts of the field have I given him also to serve him. And all nations shall serve him, and his son, and his son's son, until the very time of his land come: and then many nations and great kings shall serve themselves of him" (Jer. 27:6–7). In other words, the Babylonian kingdom would last through the reign of a son and a grandson of Nebuchadnezzar, and then the reign of the Babylonian kingdom as the head of gold would end.

We have further evidence of Belshazzar from a prayer of Nabonidus to the moon god for his son which was discovered on a clay cylinder: "My son, the offspring of my heart, might honor his godhead and not give himself to sin." Herodotus, the Greek historian, also mentions this and confirms it.

During the time of the events recorded in chapter 5, Nabonidus was on the field of battle while Belshazzar his son remained in Babylon. We will notice that when Belshazzar offers Daniel a position in the kingdom, it is to be the third ruler in the kingdom. Why not second to Belshazzar? Well, Belshazzar himself was number two—his father was really the king.

During the feast of Belshazzar introduced here in verse 1, Gobryas, the Median general, was besieging the city of Babylon from without.

Xenophon, the Greek historian, describes how they took the city by detouring a canal of the Euphrates River back into its main channel and then letting the army flow under the walls of the city.

Therefore the events of this chapter, which for many years had been discounted by the critics, have today been confirmed by secular history. I would rather say that secular history has been confirmed by the Word of God. We know that historians are sometimes liars, and we cannot always depend upon their writings. However, here the historical research does agree with the account of Scripture.

"Belshazzar the king made a great feast to a thousand of his lords, and drank wine before the thousand." Note the arrogance of this young upstart Belshazzar who puts on this lavish affair while the armies of Gobryas were in full view of the city. Perhaps Belshazzar thought the city was impregnable. Nebuchadnezzar had built it to withstand any siege. The city wall was actually fifteen miles square and was constructed of brick. It was three hundred feet high and wide enough for four chariots to travel abreast around the city walls. In other words, they could have put a freeway around the top of the city. He had supplies of grain and water to last for years—in fact, there was a canal channeled off the Euphrates River which went right through the city.

Belshazzar's feast may have been in defiance of the enemy on the outside, or perhaps he wanted to build up the morale of those within. We are told here that it began with a big cocktail party.

Liquor today is a temporary prop for weak men and women, and alcohol is still the number one drug problem in the United States. I thought it rather ironical when a group of well-meaning citizens in Los Angeles—leaders from the schools, the churches, and politics—met together to discuss the drug problem among young people. You know how they opened their meeting? With a cocktail party! How hypocritical can you be? My friend, there are far more alcoholics in this country than drug addicts. Do you know that more than half of those killed in traffic accidents each year have alcohol in their blood at the time of the accident? Many billions of dollars are spent annually by Americans for alcoholic beverages. Alcohol is doing great damage—in automobile accidents and in homes being absolutely wrecked. The liquor problem is an alarming problem, and it is a problem common to all of mankind. Many nations have gone down because of liquor—and not because of marijuana. Don't misunderstand me—I am not supporting the use of marijuana. I just cannot get enthusiastic about these reformers who want to solve the drug problem but will not give up their alcohol; I don't care for that hypocrisy.

Old Belshazzar started off with a big cocktail party to get his guests high so they would enjoy the banquet that he was going to put on for them.

> **Belshazzar, whiles he tasted the wine, commanded to bring the golden and silver vessels which his father Nebuchadnezzar had taken out of the temple which was in Jerusalem; that the king, and his princes, his wives, and his concubines, might drink therein.**
>
> **Then they brought the golden vessels that were taken out of the temple of the house of God which was at Jerusalem; and the king, and his princes, his wives, and his concubines, drank in them [Dan. 5:2-3].**

This man is not only defying the enemy outside, but now under the influence of alcohol he does an audacious thing which his grandfather would never have done. When Nebuchadnezzar took Jerusalem, he was an old, pagan, heathen king, and he took the vessels from the temple in Jerusalem. But when he came to the knowledge of the living and true God, he had them stored away. To Belshazzar as a boy growing up in the palace, I guess they were a no-no—he had to leave those vessels alone. Now he drags them out and is going to serve his guests with them.

The vessels were no longer holy vessels. Holy means "that which is set aside for the use of God." However, Belshazzar is defying God by this act. And men today are defying God by their actions. We are prompted to speak out and to wonder why God doesn't deal with such people. My friend, God has plenty of time. He will take care of the situation, just as He is going to take care of Belshazzar.

Belshazzar knew that his grandfather had come to the knowledge of God and had praised and honored Him (see v. 22); yet he deliberately defied and profaned God. Proverbs 29:1 says, "He, that being often reproved hardeneth his neck, shall suddenly be destroyed, and that without remedy."

Everyone at the banquet was now beastly drunk. It was a scene of real debauchery and licentiousness. Ever since I was a boy, I have heard preachers preach on this banquet of Belshazzar—it must have been a real banquet according to some of them! One of the preachers talked about the dancing girls and the drinking and the laughter and all that sort of thing. If the truth were told, the sermon was like a vicarious trip to a nightclub, and we all enjoyed it. However, Scripture gives us no such details.

They drank wine, and praised the gods of gold, and of silver, of brass, of iron, of wood, and of stone [Dan. 5:4].

They toasted the gods, and it would have taken more than one night to toast all they had in Babylon. They cloaked their sin as an act of worship and veiled their blasphemy in the name of religion.

FINGERS OF GOD WRITE UPON THE WALL

In the same hour came forth fingers of a man's hand, and wrote over against the candlestick upon the plaster of the wall of the king's palace: and the king saw the part of the hand that wrote [Dan. 5:5].

God now directly intervenes. He does not speak by dream or vision because this is a man whom He doesn't intend to reach. God would not endure this impious insult to heaven, so He writes on the wall of the banqueting hall. Is it done in anger? Very frankly, I think it is, and I believe the One who wrote this is the same One who wrote in the sand when they brought a sinful woman before Him (John 8:1–11). At that time it was a message of forgiveness; here, for Belshazzar, it is a message of doom. He has ignored the God of heaven, as Daniel will soon make clear to him.

Then the king's countenance was changed, and his thoughts troubled him, so that the joints of his loins were loosed, and his knees smote one against another [Dan. 5:6].

Belshazzar couldn't stand up. A few moments ago he had been too drunk to stand up. Although he's suddenly sober he still cannot stand up. What he has seen on the wall has scared him nearly to death; he is overwhelmed with fear.

The king cried aloud to bring in the astrologers, the Chaldeans, and the soothsayers. And the king spake, and said to the wise men of Babylon, Whosoever shall read this writing, and shew me the interpretation thereof, shall be clothed with scarlet, and have a chain of gold about his neck, and shall be the third ruler in the kingdom [Dan. 5:7].

Notice that the reward was to be "the third ruler in the kingdom." How accurate Daniel is! The man who wrote this book had to have been there and understood the circumstances: Nabonidus was the real king, and Belshazzar was only second in the kingdom.

FAILURE OF THE WISE MEN TO READ THE HANDWRITING

Then came in all the king's wise men: but they could not read the writing, nor make known to the king the interpretation thereof [Dan. 5:8].

When Belshazzar finally got his senses back he had the wise men trotted in, and he asked them to give the interpretation of the writing on the wall. Although he offered them a handsome reward, they could only stand there looking at him. They didn't know the answer, and they didn't know what to do. This is the third time the wise men of Babylon have failed. On the third strike, you're out, you know—I think maybe this incident put them out of business.

> **Then was king Belshazzar greatly troubled, and his countenance was changed in him, and his lords were astonied [Dan. 5:9].**

You can imagine the change which took place in that banquet room. A few moments before they all had been laughing and drunk. Now they are sober and perplexed and troubled.

> **Now the queen, by reason of the words of the king and his lords, came into the banquet house: and the queen spake and said, O king, live for ever: let not thy thoughts trouble thee, nor let thy countenance be changed [Dan.5:10].**

The "queen" here is the queen mother, the wife of Nebuchadnezzar. She heard what had happened at the banquet, and she came in to speak to the king.

> **There is a man in thy kingdom, in whom is the spirit of the holy gods; and in the days of thy father light and understanding and wisdom, like the wisdom of the gods, was found in him; whom the king Nebuchadnezzar thy father, the king, I say, thy father, made master of the magicians, astrologers, Chaldeans, and soothsayers [Dan. 5:11].**

"Nebuchadnezzar thy father"—relationships were indicated with one word; therefore "father" could refer to a father, a grandfather, a great-grandfather, or a great-great-grandfather.

> **Forasmuch as an excellent spirit, and knowledge, and understanding, interpreting of dreams, and shewing of hard sentences, and dissolving of doubts, were found in the same Daniel, whom the king named Belteshazzar:**

now let Daniel be called, and he will shew the interpretation [Dan. 5:12].

The queen mother has come to help her grandson out of his predicament. She tells him there is a man in his kingdom by the name of Daniel, a Spirit-filled man, who can decipher the writing.

DANIEL SPURNS THE KING'S GIFTS

Then was Daniel brought in before the king. And the king spake and said unto Daniel, Art thou that Daniel, which art of the children of the captivity of Judah, whom the king my father brought out of Jewry?

I have even heard of thee, that the spirit of the gods is in thee, and that light and understanding and excellent wisdom is found in thee [Dan. 5:13-14].

Daniel is now brought in. He evidently had been set aside and pushed out of office after the death of Nebuchadnezzar.

And now the wise men, the astrologers, have been brought in before me, that they should read this writing, and make known unto me the interpretation thereof: but they could not shew the interpretation of the thing:

And I have heard of thee, that thou canst make interpretations, and dissolve doubts: now if thou canst read the writing, and make known to me the interpretation thereof, thou shalt be clothed with scarlet, and have a chain of gold about thy neck, and shalt be the third ruler in the kingdom [Dan. 5:15-16].

Belshazzar butters him up and tells him that if he can give the interpretation which the wise men have failed to give, then he will be made the third ruler in the kingdom. Thus Daniel is offered the same reward which had been offered to the wise men.

> **Then Daniel answered and said before the king, Let thy gifts be to thyself, and give thy rewards to another; yet I will read the writing unto the king, and make known to him the interpretation [Dan. 5:17].**

Daniel spurned these gifts. He was absolutely contemptuous of Belshazzar. I am sure that if the king had not been so filled with fear, he would not have ignored Daniel's insult. After all, why did Daniel need this reward? He would not have had it but for a few hours.

Before Daniel interprets the handwriting on the wall, he gives to this young king who is reigning under his father the best sermon he probably ever could receive. Daniel is not the young man who went into the presence of old King Nebuchadnezzar; he is now an old man going into the presence of a young king. There had been no generation gap with Nebuchadnezzar, and there is not one now. Listen to what Daniel tells Belshazzar:

> **O thou king, the most high God gave Nebuchadnezzar thy father a kingdom, and majesty, and glory, and honour:**
>
> **And for the majesty that he gave him, all people, nations, and languages, trembled and feared before him: whom he would he slew; and whom he would he kept alive; and whom he would he set up; and whom he would he put down [Dan. 5:18–19].**

Nebuchadnezzar had been an absolute ruler on this earth. I believe there has not been another ruler like him and there will not be another until Antichrist rules. Daniel recites for Belshazzar how God had dealt with his grandfather. God had put him on the throne and had given him a world kingdom. Then he tells Belshazzar of the experience Nebuchadnezzar had had:

But when his heart was lifted up, and his mind hardened in pride, he was deposed from his kingly throne, and they took his glory from him:

And he was driven from the sons of men; and his heart was made like the beasts, and his dwelling was with the wild asses: they fed him with grass like oxen, and his body was wet with the dew of heaven; till he knew that the most high God ruled in the kingdom of men, and that he appointeth over it whomsoever he will.

And thou his son, O Belshazzar, hast not humbled thine heart, though thou knewest all this;

But hast lifted up thyself against the Lord of heaven; and they have brought the vessels of his house before thee, and thou, and thy lords, thy wives, and thy concubines, have drunk wine in them; and thou hast praised the gods of silver, and gold, of brass, iron, wood, and stone, which see not, nor hear, nor know: and the God in whose hand thy breath is, and whose are all thy ways, hast thou not glorified:

Then was the part of the hand sent from him; and this writing was written [Dan. 5:20–24].

Daniel preaches a very pointed and powerful sermon to Belshazzar. God had given the kingdom to Nebuchadnezzar, and he had been an absolute sovereign whom no man could question or hinder and whose wishes and whims were the law of the realm. However, when Nebuchadnezzar became filled with pride, God humbled him to a tragic episode. When Daniel reminds Belshazzar of Nebuchadnezzar's humiliating experience, you wonder if Daniel is rubbing it in. Perhaps he is. He is reminding this young proud king that if he is lifted up by pride, it is either because of his drinking or because he is insane.

Belshazzar was a proud and vain man. Although he knew of his grandfather's insanity and of his descent to the level of a beast, he had not profited by this experience. Instead, he had committed sacrilege in using the vessels taken from God's temple in Jerusalem. He had defied the living and true God; and, by the profane use of that which had been holy, he had mocked God and insulted Him. Knowing the truth, he yet rejected it.

God destroys only those who have known the truth and have refused it. During the Great Tribulation period those who will be deluded are those who have rejected the light. Paul writes in 2 Thessalonians 2:9-12, "Even him, whose coming is after the working of Satan with all power and signs and lying wonders, And with all deceivableness of unrighteousness in them that perish; because they received not the love of the truth, that they might be saved. And for this cause God shall send them strong delusion, that they should believe a lie: That they all might be damned who believed not the truth, but had pleasure in unrighteousness." Daniel is telling Belshazzar the principle by which God operates and which Paul has also since confirmed. The Lord Jesus also made this very clear when He said: "I am come in my Father's name, and ye receive me not: if another shall come in his own name, him ye will receive" (John 5:43).

The people in Germany who accepted Hitler were the same people that had rejected the Word of God in Christ. When you turn your back on the truth, you are wide open for any cult or ism which comes along. Why is it that cults and isms are growing today? Why is it that we hear so much about demonism and the worship of Satan? These things are being manifested in our nation because it is a nation that has had the Word of God and has rejected it.

We desperately need the *teaching* of the Word of God. We have enough preaching—we have enough people telling us what they think. What does God say? What difference does it make what you or I think? What God thinks—that is what is important.

Daniel concludes his sermon by stating that the handwriting was from God whom Belshazzar had spurned and ridiculed and blasphemed. Some people wonder if he had committed an unpardonable sin. I'll let you answer that. I just know that he had an opportunity here to receive the truth, and he turned it down.

DANIEL INTERPRETS THE HANDWRITING ON THE WALL

And this is the writing that was written, MENE, MENE, TEKEL, UPHARSIN [Dan. 5:25].

I can't resist telling you the story of a man who was a foreigner in this country and was finally persuaded by his daughter to go to church, although he had great difficulty understanding English. However, he agreed to go with his daughter, Minnie, on the Sunday the preacher had unfortunately chosen for his text the account of this writing on the wall: MENE, MENE, TEKEL, UPHARSIN. As soon as the preacher mentioned this, the man grabbed Minnie his daughter by the hand and took her out of the church. "Father, what in the world is the matter?" she asked. With a very heavy accent, he replied, "Did you hear what the preacher said? He said, 'Minnie, Minnie, come tickle the parson'!" Well, that is not the interpretation of this writing upon Belshazzar's wall. Daniel gives the interpretation:

This is the interpretation of the thing: MENE; God hath numbered thy kingdom, and finished it [Dan. 5:26].

MENE is translated "number," and it is repeated—Number, Number. It meant that God had numbered the kingdom of Babylon. We have a common colloquialism today, "His number is up." That is an accurate expression of the idea here. Also, in Psalm 90:12, we read, "So teach us to number our days, that we may apply our hearts unto wisdom." Only God knows when "our number is up"—when our earthly journey is over.

There was a young man who had never flown on a plane before, and his friends were encouraging him to take a trip to California. Well, he didn't want to go because he was afraid the plane might go down. His friends assured him, "It doesn't matter where you are—if your number's up, it's up—whether you're on a plane or not." But the boy said, "I'm not worried about my number being up. I just worry whether it's time for the *pilot's* number to be up. If it is, I'd rather not be on that plane!"

"MENE, MENE" means that God had numbered the days of the Babylonian kingdom. He keeps track of every moment of every day. He determines beforehand the length of our days, and we cannot change that.

TEKEL; Thou art weighed in the balances, and art found wanting [Dan. 5:27].

TEKEL simply means "weight." Babylon had been put on the divine scales and had been found wanting. The people of Babylon didn't weigh enough—they were lightweight. God had raised up Babylon, and now He is going to put it down. Why? Because Babylon had not measured up to God's standards.

We read in the second and third chapters of the Book of Revelation about the seven churches of Asia Minor. There we see the Lord Jesus in the midst of the lampstands which represent the churches. He trims the wicks, pours in the oil, and snuffs out those which fail to light. He also judges the church today. Now we may weigh out at sixteen ounces to the pound on the Toledo scales we have down here, but Christ weighs us on the divine scale, and He had to say to every one of the churches, "Repent. You haven't measured up." He says the same thing to you and me today. Our righteousness is not only insufficient, it is filthy rags. Only His righteousness is going to stand the test and weigh out at sixteen ounces to the pound. Romans 3:21–23 says, "But now the righteousness of God without the law is manifested, being witnessed by the law and the prophets; Even the righteousness of God which is by faith of Jesus Christ unto all upon all them that believe: for there is no difference: For all have sinned, and come short of the glory of God." You see, God weighs the actions of mankind.

PERES; Thy kingdom is divided, and given to the Medes and Persians [Dan. 5:28].

PERES is the singular form of *UPHARSIN* (as it was given in verse 25), and it means "divisions." The kingdom of Babylon is now to be di-

vided and given to the Medes and Persians. In other words, the head of
gold is to be removed; it is now time for the arms of silver to come into
place. God is in supreme command of the kingdoms of the earth. Ezekiel wrote, "I will overturn, overturn, overturn, it: and it shall be no
more, until he come whose right it is; and I will give it him" (Ezek.
21:27). God will continue to turn over kingdoms until Christ comes. I
think He is doing a pretty good job. I remember a few years ago when
Mussolini and Hitler and Stalin were real terrors to the world—all that
crowd is gone now. God is still in charge, and Christ is that "stone . . .
cut out without hands" (Dan. 2:34) who is going to establish His
Kingdom down here someday.

> **Then commanded Belshazzar, and they clothed Daniel
> with scarlet, and put a chain of gold about his neck, and
> made a proclamation concerning him, that he should be
> the third ruler in the kingdom [Dan. 5:29].**

Again, note that it is "the third ruler in the kingdom." How accurate
the Book of Daniel is. Nabonidus was really the king, and Belshazzar,
the grandson of Nebuchadnezzar, was second in command.

FALL OF BABYLON—FULFILLMENT THAT VERY NIGHT

> **In that night was Belshazzar the king of the Chaldeans
> slain.**

> **And Darius the Median took the kingdom, being about
> threescore and two years old [Dan. 5:30–31].**

At the very time this banquet was being held, the Medes were
marching underneath the walls of Babylon where the waters of the
canal had flowed. As I mentioned earlier, underneath the wall of that
city had been a canal which had brought water through the city, and
now the waters had been cut off and channeled back into the main
stream of the Euphrates River. This man Gobryas was marching his

army into the inner city where the palace was located. History records that he and his men were on the inside of the inner city before the guards had even detected that anything was wrong. It is Xenophon, the Greek historian, who recorded for secular history the way in which the Persians took the city.

Belshazzar was slain—he had been weighed and found wanting. God does that, and He uses His scale and His standards. He says to you and me, ". . . all have sinned, and come short of the glory of God" (Rom. 3:23). You and I are not 100 percent wool, a yard wide and warranted not to wrinkle or unravel. We just do not measure up to God's standard. We are not on trial today; we are lost, and God is offering us salvation. Belshazzar had rejected God, and he was slain.

Darius the Median became the ruler of the kingdom of silver. He came with a sudden attack and destroyed Babylon. Isaiah had prophesied the fall of Babylon in Isaiah 21. In a future day another Babylon will fall by the hands of God (see Rev. 18)—thus will end man's vaunted civilization.

CHAPTER 6

THEME: Position of Daniel under Darius the Mede;
plot to destroy Daniel; prayer of Daniel; Daniel in
the den of lions; Daniel's deliverance; prosperity of
Daniel and the decree of Darius

Chapter 6 of the Book of Daniel is perhaps one of the most familiar in the Bible and certainly is the most well-known of this book. It is the account of Daniel in the den of lions. Have you ever stopped to think that Daniel spent only one night in the den of lions, but he spent a lifetime—from a boy of seventeen until he was about ninety—in the palace of pagan kings? It was more dangerous to live in that palace than it was to spend a night in the den of lions. The lions could not touch him, but yonder in the palace of Nebuchadnezzar, Nabonidus, Belshazzar, Darius the Median, and Cyrus, who were pagan men, Daniel was in constant danger. However, he had the privilege of leading some of these men to a knowledge of the living and true God.

Daniel spent only one night in the den of lions, but we are going to look at it because it has a message for us today. This chapter concludes the strictly historical section of the Book of Daniel, and each historical event has been recorded for us for a purpose. This particular episode in Daniel's life is another illustration of the keeping of the power of God, and it is another adumbration of the way in which God will protect the remnant during the Great Tribulation period. This chapter is a counterpart of chapter 3 where God preserved Daniel's three friends in the fiery furnace. As there was a question as to the whereabouts of Daniel in chapter 3, there is also a question as to the whereabouts of the three Hebrew children here in chapter 6. Surely they would have followed Daniel in his obedience to God. Perhaps, since there has been a lapse of time, they are no longer living.

Chapters 3 and 6, therefore, give two aspects of the preservation of the remnant—both of Israel and of the Gentiles—during the Great Tribulation period. In chapter 3 the emphasis is upon the pressures

which are brought to bear by human hatred and persecution. In this
chapter the emphasis is rather upon satanic hatred and persecution.
The message for us today is, "Be sober, be vigilant; because your adversary the devil, as a roaring lion, walketh about, seeking whom he
may devour" (1 Pet. 5:8). You and I live in a lion's cage. That cage is
the world, and there is a big roaring lion prowling up and down the
cage. Peter calls him our adversary, the Devil.

POSITION OF DANIEL UNDER DARIUS THE MEDE

**It pleased Darius to set over the kingdom an hundred
and twenty princes, which should be over the whole
kingdom;**

**And over these three presidents; of whom Daniel was
first: that the princes might give accounts unto them,
and the king should have no damage [Dan. 6:1–2].**

With the opening of this chapter, we have again moved ahead historically. The kingdom of Babylon, the head of gold, has now disappeared; it has been removed from the number one spot of world
power. Instead of Babylon, we have the Medo-Persian Empire, which
was represented by the arms of silver in the dream of Nebuchadnezzar.
"Darius" is the Darius Cyaxares II of secular history, and he ruled for
only two years. Cyrus, who followed him, was the son of Darius' sister
Mundane and of Cambyses the Persian. This was what brought the
empire together into the Medo-Persian Empire which now ruled the
world.

Although we have moved into another empire, we still find Daniel
in the position of prime minister under Darius the Mede. When we
were considering the multimetallic image of gold, silver, brass, iron,
and clay (ch. 2), we suggested that it pictured deterioration in a number of ways. There was deterioration in position, in the type of metal,
etc. Here we can see that the inferiority of this kingdom to Nebuchadnezzar's is quite evident. Nebuchadnezzar's reign was autocratic and
absolute—he did not share authority with anyone. Darius had "an

hundred and twenty princes" who shared the responsibility and leadership with him. Over this group Darius placed "three presidents" who served as liaison officers between the princes and the king. There was therefore a distribution of responsibility and rulership. We are told that these three presidents (Daniel was one of them) held their position so that "the king should have no damage." This suggests that the presidents were to prevent the princes from stealing from or undermining the king in any way. Daniel was number one of the three presidents, and I take it that he was a man of about eighty years of age at this time.

> **Then this Daniel was preferred above the presidents and princes, because an excellent spirit was in him; and the king thought to set him over the whole realm [Dan. 6:3].**

Daniel not only had seniority in this group, he had superiority. That he possessed "an excellent spirit" means Daniel was a Spirit-filled man. The king had such confidence in him that he placed Daniel next to himself in position and power.

PLOT TO DESTROY DANIEL

> **Then the presidents and princes sought to find occasion against Daniel concerning the kingdom; but they could find none occasion nor fault; forasmuch as he was faithful, neither was there any error or fault found in him [Dan. 6:4].**

One thing is for sure: When you find yourself the number one man in any position—whether it be in church, in politics, in school, or even in the home—you are the one who will be watched by those who have a jealous spirit. If there is a flaw in your life, if you have an Achilles' heel, they are going to discover that weak spot and may use it against you.

Now Daniel had a remarkable life behind him. These men could not find anything in this man's character or in his past life which they could seize upon and make something of. There has been many a politician who wished he had lived and acted a little differently—actually, that could be said of mankind generally.

Today a child of God ought to live so that the charges which inevitably will be leveled against him will be a lie. You cannot keep people from talking about you, but you can live so as to make them liars when they do talk about you. The apostle Paul enjoins all believers, "That ye may be blameless and harmless, the sons of God, without rebuke, in the midst of a crooked and perverse nation, among whom ye shine as lights in the world" (Phil. 2:15). This was Paul's personal testimony— "And herein do I exercise myself, to have always a conscience void of offence toward God, and toward men" (Acts 24:16). In other words, Paul could lie down at night and go to sleep, and he did not have a bad conscience troubling him. That ought to be true of every believer. Someone has said that a conscience is something that only a good man can enjoy.

> **Then said these men, We shall not find any occasion against this Daniel, except we find it against him concerning the law of his God [Dan. 6:5].**

Daniel was different—God had made His people different. When he was first brought to the court of Nebuchadnezzar as a boy slave, he had asked for a different diet. From then on, the life of Daniel was different, and these men were aware of that. They said, "If we are going to find anything wrong with him, we are going to have to find it in his religion." When they said "wrong," they meant something which they could accuse him of before the king. The only vulnerable spot in Daniel, as these politicians saw it, was his religion. This was certainly a case of Daniel's good being "evil-spoken of." They knew that Daniel was faithful to God and was dependent upon Him. His prayer life was something that was well known. Therefore, they are going to have to draw a conflict between the king and Daniel's religion.

> **Then these presidents and princes assembled together to the king, and said thus unto him, King Darius, live for ever.**

All the presidents of the kingdom, the governors, and the princes, the counsellors, and the captains, have consulted together to establish a royal statute, and to make a firm decree, that whosoever shall ask a petition of any God or man for thirty days, save of thee, O king, he shall be cast into the den of lions [Dan. 6:6-7].

The plot of these princes and presidents and petty politicians was very subtle. King Darius was a good man. That is obvious from secular history, and I think it is certainly the implication of the Book of Daniel. But Darius had a vulnerable spot (many of us have it), and that was his vanity—he yielded to flattery.

One of the tragedies of our day is that there are many Christians, especially of financial means, who give only to organizations where the leader of the organization flatters them and butters them up. It is my conviction that we do not need to stoop to flattering people to get them to contribute financially to a ministry; God will speak to people's hearts if He wants them to support a ministry.

A long time ago I discovered that I am not as bad as my enemies say and I am not nearly as good as my friends say that I am. There is always a danger of being carried away by flattery. I used to tell my students in seminary, "Fellows, it does not matter how poor a preacher you are or what church you are in, the Lord will always have some dear lady who will tell you how wonderful you are. She will come up to you after you have preached the lousiest sermon in the world, and she will tell you, 'My, I think you are another Dwight L. Moody on the scene!' It is nice to have such dear ladies who want to encourage you like that, but just don't believe them. There is a danger if you do."

These men flattered Darius, and he yielded to it. He thought, *My, this is great!* So he drafted a bill, and it was made a statute. He thus elevated himself to the position of deity, and prayer was to be offered only to him.

Now, O king, establish the decree, and sign the writing, that it be not changed, according to the law of the Medes and Persians, which altereth not.

Wherefore King Darius signed the writing and the decree [Dan. 6:8-9].

Darius yielded to his weakness, and now this decree which has gone out, signed by the king, cannot be changed. Even the king of the Medes and Persians himself cannot change it after it has been passed. All this puts Daniel in a bad spot.

PRAYER OF DANIEL

Now when Daniel knew that the writing was signed, he went into his house; and his windows being open in his chamber toward Jerusalem, he kneeled upon his knees three times a day, and prayed, and gave thanks before his God, as he did aforetime [Dan. 6:10].

Notice the reaction of Daniel to this new law. He did not do anything audacious or foolhardy when he opened those windows—he had been doing that for years. He simply did not back down. He did not act in a cowardly and compromising manner by closing the windows but went about his usual prayer life.

I would like to note that he kneeled to pray. The proper posture is often a question. I really doubt that the posture of prayer is the important thing. Victor Hugo said that the soul is on its knees many times regardless of the position of the body. The posture of the spirit of the man is what is important. However, if you want to select a posture for prayer, it is kneeling, and that is set before us here.

Notice also that Daniel prayed toward Jerusalem. That was the direction of Daniel's life, and he didn't intend to change because of Darius' decree. When away from the temple in Jerusalem, God's people of that day were to pray facing in that direction. Today, no earthly place is preferred above another; the Lord Jesus said, ". . . ye shall neither in this mountain, nor yet at Jerusalem, worship the Father . . . . God is a Spirit: and they that worship him must worship him in spirit and in truth" (John 4:21, 24).

> Then these men assembled, and found Daniel praying
> and making supplication before his God [Dan. 6:11].

These men were waiting for Daniel, and that was really a compliment.
This man had a reputation, and they had a feeling that he would not
back down from his convictions.

> Then they came near, and spake before the king con-
> cerning the king's decree; Hast thou not signed a de-
> cree, that every man that shall ask a petition of any God
> or man within thirty days, save of thee, O king, shall be
> cast into the den of lions? The king answered and said,
> The thing is true, according to the law of the Medes and
> Persians, which altereth not.
>
> Then answered they and said before the king, That Dan-
> iel, which is of the children of the captivity of Judah,
> regardeth not thee, O king, nor the decree that thou hast
> signed, but maketh his petition three times a day.
>
> Then the king, when he heard these words, was sore
> displeased with himself, and set his heart on Daniel to
> deliver him: and he laboured till the going down of the
> sun to deliver him [Dan. 6:12–14].

These men called attention to the fact that Daniel was disobeying: he
was at an open window praying toward Jerusalem. Believe me, this
was something which distressed the king. Darius could not change
his own law; Nebuchadnezzar would have been able to. This is evidence of the deterioration from one kingdom to the next.

> Then these men assembled unto the king, and said unto
> the king, Know, O king, that the law of the Medes and
> Persians is, That no decree nor statute which the king
> establisheth may be changed [Dan. 6:15].

Daniel is to be put in the den of lions, and there is nothing the king can do about it.

DANIEL IN THE DEN OF LIONS

Then the king commanded and they brought Daniel, and cast him into the den of lions. Now the king spake and said unto Daniel, Thy God whom thou servest continually, he will deliver thee [Dan. 6:16].

I am of the opinion that the king did not believe what he said. It was like one of the halfhearted things some of us saints say today. We tell someone else, "Oh, the Lord will take care of you," but if we were in that predicament, we wouldn't quite trust Him like that. King Darius, though, had come a long way. He recognized that the God of Daniel was omnipotent and sovereign and could deliver him. He also saw that Daniel was faithful to God. Daniel's testimony in the dissolute court of two world powers was nothing short of miraculous. His unaffected and unassuming life was a powerful witness to the saving grace of God in that day.

And a stone was brought, and laid upon the mouth of the den; and the king sealed it with his own signet, and with the signet of his lords; that the purpose might not be changed concerning Daniel [Dan. 6:17].

They put a stone against the mouth of the den of lions, and Daniel spent the night down there. These lions were fierce and wild beasts—they were not toothless old lions.

There is the story about the man who got a job at a zoo, and he was asked to go into the lions' cage to feed the lions. When he refused, the keeper said, "Look, those lions are toothless!" The man replied, "Yes, I noticed that, but they could gum me to death."

Daniel's lions had teeth, and they were fierce, but the safest place that night just happened to be the den of lions. I think Daniel got a pretty good night's sleep down there. The interesting thing is that the king was more disturbed than Daniel and was probably in more danger.

DANIEL'S DELIVERANCE

Then the king went to his palace, and passed the night fasting: neither were instruments of music brought before him: and his sleep went from him [Dan. 6:18].

The king didn't sleep, but Daniel did! Darius passed a sleepless night due to his concern for Daniel.

Then the king arose very early in the morning, and went in haste unto the den of lions.

And when he came to the den, he cried with a lamentable voice unto Daniel: and the king spake and said to Daniel, O Daniel, servant of the living God, is thy God, whom thou servest continually, able to deliver thee from the lions? [Dan. 6:19–20].

I don't know if the king expected Daniel to answer, but Daniel answered:

Then said Daniel unto the king, O king, live for ever.

My God hath sent his angel, and hath shut the lions' mouths, that they have not hurt me: forasmuch as before him innocency was found in me; and also before thee, O king, have I done no hurt [Dan. 6:21–22].

"O king, live for ever" was Daniel's polite and respectful greeting. It was as if Daniel said, "Did you have a good night?" And of course, the king hadn't had a good night, but Daniel had.

Daniel evidently had been given the same assurance as had his three friends in the fiery furnace that God could and would deliver him. "His angel" was evidently the same One Nebuchadnezzar had seen in the fiery furnace—the preincarnate Christ Himself.

Then was the king exceeding glad for him, and commanded that they should take Daniel up out of the den. So Daniel was taken up out of the den, and no manner of hurt was found upon him, because he believed in his God [Dan. 6:23].

The king loved Daniel and was sincerely delighted at his preservation. Daniel was saved by faith: "Who through faith subdued kingdoms, wrought righteousness, obtained promises, *stopped the mouths of lions*" (Heb. 11:33, italics mine).

And the king commanded, and they brought those men which had accused Daniel, and they cast them into the den of lions, them, their children, and their wives; and the lions had the mastery of them, and brake all their bones in pieces or ever they came at the bottom of the den [Dan. 6:24].

The dastardly plot of those who were enemies of Daniel was uncovered. Together with their families, they were cast into the dens of lions. The viciousness of the lions is now demonstrated in all its hideousness.

PROSPERITY OF DANIEL AND
THE DECREE OF DARIUS

Then king Darius wrote unto all people, nations, and languages, that dwell in all the earth; Peace be multiplied unto you [Dan. 6:25].

Darius sent out a worldwide decree which was his personal testimony. He had found the same peace that had come to Nebuchadnezzar (see Dan. 4:1). This testimony of peace comes from the same man who could not sleep the night before.

> **I make a decree, That in every dominion of my kingdom men tremble and fear before the God of Daniel: for he is the living God, and stedfast for ever, and his kingdom that which shall not be destroyed, and his dominion shall be even unto the end.**

> **He delivereth and rescueth, and he worketh signs and wonders in heaven and in earth, who hath delivered Daniel from the power of the lions [Dan. 6:26–27].**

Darius commands men to fear the God of Daniel and testifies that He is the living God (in contrast to idols) and that He is sovereign. Darius was brought to God through the miracle of the den of lions.

> **So this Daniel prospered in the reign of Darius, and in the reign of Cyrus the Persian [Dan. 6:28].**

Daniel's position was secure, and he maintained it to the end of his life which came during the reign of Cyrus. It was Cyrus who made the decree permitting the Jews to return to Palestine (see 2 Chron. 36:22–23; Ezra 1:11).

This concludes the strictly historical section of the Book of Daniel. From this point on the book will be mainly concerned with the visions and prophecies which were given to Daniel over the long period of his life spent in a foreign land.

CHAPTER 7

THEME: *Daniel's vision of the four beasts; the visions of the Son of Man coming in clouds of heaven; the definition of the four beasts; the explanation of the fourth beast*

Chapter 7 opens a new and different section of the Book of Daniel. The first six chapters contained the historic night with prophetic light; the last six chapters are prophetic light in the historic night. Whereas in the first section of the book the emphasis was upon the historical, the emphasis will now be on the prophetic, yet still with an historical background.

God gives to Daniel several visions of four beasts which are quite remarkable. Daniel had these visions at different periods. The vision of chapter 7 was in the first year of King Belshazzar. In chapter 8 the vision was seen in the third year of the reign of Belshazzar. In chapter 9 it was in the first year of Darius; in chapter 10 it was the third year of Cyrus; and in chapters 11 and 12 the vision was seen in the first year of Darius. Daniel did not record these visions in the historical section but gathered these prophetic visions together in this second section of his book.

DANIEL'S VISION OF THE FOUR BEASTS

Nebuchadnezzar of Babylon was a very brilliant man who found himself suddenly elevated to the position of the first great world ruler. He had territory on three continents. He had taken Egypt in North Africa, and he also had territory in Europe. He had a tremendous empire, greater than any the world had ever known. But Nebuchadnezzar wondered about the future: What would happen to him and to his empire? He dreamed a dream about a multimetallic image, and through Daniel God gave the interpretation of the dream (see Dan. 2).

There were *four* different kinds of metals in Nebuchadnezzar's image—not five, but four metals. Daniel's vision of the beasts is of *four* beasts—the lion, the bear, the panther (or leopard), and a composite beast which has been called a nondescript beast. The last was a wild-looking animal which has never been seen on land or sea or in the air—it simply does not exist as a real beast. Well, after he had had visions and dreams like that, I don't think Daniel slept much that night. He probably got a better night's sleep in the den of lions than he did the night he had this dream!

I imagine that, after God gave him Nebuchadnezzar's dream and its interpretation, Daniel was quite puzzled. As a good student and follower of the Old Testament, Daniel knew of the covenant which God had made with David—that One was coming in his line who would be a world ruler. Now with the four world kingdoms of Nebuchadnezzar's dream before him, he wondered how God's plan and program of raising up a world ruler from David would fit into all this. The rest of the Book of Daniel is going to answer that question. It will give us world history prewritten, history that has been followed right down to the minutest detail for twenty-five hundred years since the time it was written.

God speaks to Daniel through his vision of the four beasts to satisfy his heart and to give him the explanation he needed. In Daniel's vision of the multimetallic image the outward splendor and glory of the kingdoms was demonstrated—that was what God knew would attract Nebuchadnezzar's attention. But in the vision He gives to Daniel, God lets him in on the inward character and the true nature of these kingdoms. What are these kingdoms? These are like wild beasts, carnivorous in nature, and destructive killers every one of them.

The four beasts of Daniel's vision of course correspond to the four metals in the image of Nebuchadnezzar's vision. In *The Decline and Fall of the Roman Empire*, the historian Edward Gibbon, who was not a Christian, said, "The four empires are clearly delineated; and the invincible armies of the Romans are described with as much clearness in the prophecies of Daniel, as in the histories of Justin and Diodorus." The following chart summarizes the correspondence between the two visions and the four kingdoms they represent:

Multimetallic Image (Chapter 2)	Four Beasts (Chapter 7)	Nations Designated
Head of Gold	Lion	Babylon
Arms of Silver	Bear	Medo-Persia
Sides of Brass	Panther (leopard)	Graeco-Macedonia
Legs of Iron; Feet of Iron and Clay	Composite beast	Rome

In the first year of Belshazzar king of Babylon Daniel had a dream and visions of his head upon his bed: then he wrote the dream, and told the sum of the matters [Dan. 7:1].

The time of this vision is pinpointed historically for us in the first year of Belshaszzar; that is, toward the end of the time that the head of gold, or Babylon, was ruling in the world. Belshazzar was reigning in Babylon the night Gobryas came with his army under the city wall, where the canal had once flowed, and took the city.

"Visions" suggests that the first three beasts are given in the first vision, the second vision concerned the fourth beast only, and the third vision is a scene in heaven. Therefore, there are actually three visions which are recorded here.

"He wrote the dream." Daniel was in obscurity in Babylon at this time, and I think he had more opportunity to give attention to the Word of God and to writing. Perhaps it was in this period that he recorded the first part of the Book of Daniel.

Daniel spake and said, I saw in my vision by night, and, behold, the four winds of the heaven strove upon the great sea [Dan. 7:2].

The four winds broke violently "upon the *great sea*," that is, upon the Mediterranean Sea, for that is the name given to it. The "winds" speak of agitation, propaganda, public opinion, and disturbance. The "sea" suggests the masses, the mob, and the peoples of the Gentiles (see Matt. 13:47; Rev. 13:1; Isa. 57:20). In Revelation we read: "And there came one of the seven angels which had the seven vials, and talked with me, saying unto me, Come hither; I will shew unto thee the judgments of the great whore that sitteth upon many waters. . . . And he saith unto me, The waters which thou sawest, where the whore sitteth, are peoples, and multitudes, and nations, and tongues" (Rev. 17:1, 15). The sea, therefore, is this conglomerate population of Gentiles throughout the world.

Customarily the wind blows from only one direction at a time, but here it is a tornado of great violence with the wind coming from all directions. It refers not only to the disturbed conditions out of which these four nations arose, but particularly to the last stage of the fourth kingdom (vv. 11, 12, 17) in which certain ideologies shall strive to capture the thinking of the disturbed masses of all nations and tribes. We are in that last stage of the fourth kingdom today. We are very close, apparently, to the time when the Roman Empire will be brought back together again. It still exists—it lives in Italy, France, Germany, Spain, and all the nations in Europe which were in the Roman Empire. All it needs is someone who will put it back together. We apparently are near that time—how near I do not think we even ought to speculate.

All these nations are to be brought back together with their different ideologies, forms of government, and viewpoints. At this point we should call attention to the deadly parallel between the circumstances herein described and our own modern world situation. This is the reason I say we are evidently drawing toward the end of the age. Entire continents are awakening today, and all are demanding a place in the sun. People who have had a primitive civilization for centuries have suddenly been catapulted into the jet age. Radios and missiles have changed the thinking of the masses. New ideologies have captured their minds, and our disturbed world is desperately trying to avoid World War III.

I wonder if you have noticed as you listen to radio and look at television today that we are being brainwashed? All kinds of propaganda are being given to us. The disturbed masses are being fed propaganda. I do not mind confessing that I am interested in giving out propaganda also—the propaganda of the Word of God. I wish that I could brainwash everyone who reads this book and make him a believer in the Lord Jesus Christ.

It is the "little horn" of this chapter who will succeed in capturing the minds of the masses. He is described as having "a mouth speaking great things" (v. 8). He is going to sell himself to the world when he appears. He will be Satan's man. The Lord Jesus said, "I am come in my Father's name, and ye receive me not: if another shall come in his own name, him ye will receive" (John 5:43).

Humanism today is glorifying mankind everywhere. They are glorifying public officials, and they are glorifying stage and screen actors (who also glorify one another). These are the people who are in control of the various media today. They have made the theater respectable, whereas it was clearly the theater which corrupted the morals of the Greeks and which is corrupting our morals today.

I hear young people talking about their "freedom," but they use the same line of talk and wear the same clothes that can be found everywhere across the country. They really have no freedom at all. People are brainwashed today. We would all be better off if we would get brainwashed with the Word of God.

This is a frightful picture and a disturbed scene that Daniel is presenting to us. Don't misunderstand me—I am not saying that what we see today is a fulfillment of prophecy. I am simply saying that the winds are beginning to blow; it may be a pretty long storm.

And four great beasts came up from the sea, diverse one from another [Dan. 7:3].

The four beasts are different kinds of beasts: the lion, the bear, the panther, and the beast with ten horns. I have never seen a beast with ten horns except in this book. These beasts represent kingdoms formed out of many peoples' tongues, tribes, and nations.

The first was like a lion, and had eagle's wings: I beheld till the wings thereof were plucked, and it was lifted up from the earth, and made stand upon the feet as a man, and a man's heart was given to it [Dan. 7:4].

The lion with eagle's wings represents Babylon in particular. King Nebuchadnezzar is intended also, as verse 17 declares that the four beasts represent four kings.

This lion had eagle's wings, and that makes it an unusual lion. These eagle's wings denote the ability that Babylon had of moving an army speeedily, which has been the secret of any great world power down through history. It was a Tennessean named Gen. Nathan Bedford Forrest who, when he was asked how to win battles, said, "The one that gets there 'the first with the most' is the one that is going to win." Nebuchadnezzar had the ability to move an army speedily, and that was the thing which brought him to world power. Such was the secret of Alexander the Great, the Roman caesars, and of course Napoleon. The coming in of the airplane was significant in World War I, and then World War II was won largely by air power. The one who can move the quickest with the greatest power will be the world ruler. This was true of Babylon in the past, and it will probably be the determining factor in the future.

"The wings thereof were plucked" evidently refers to the humbling of Nebuchadnezzar in his mental lapse and loss of identity.

"And made stand upon the feet as a man"—denotes Nebuchadnezzar's restoration. He became like a beast and acted like one, but his mind was restored, and he was brought back to sanity.

"A man's heart was given to it." I believe this refers to Nebuchadnezzar's conversion. I think he came to know the living and true God.

The lion corresponds to the head of gold, Babylon. Today she is a heap of ruins; but, as predicted by Jeremiah, those very ruins bear eloquent testimony to the outward glory that was hers. Among those ruins one can see a proud lion standing on a pedestal; it was the thing which represented that great empire. Excavation of the city of Babylon reveals the glory that was once there. The hanging gardens of Babylon were one of the seven wonders of the ancient world. Nebuchadnezzar had married a girl from the hill country, but since Babylon was built down on a plain—just like west Texas—he built the hanging gardens for her so that she wouldn't be homesick. It was a thing of great beauty. There was also a great ziggurat evidently patterned after the Tower of Babel. It was made of brick, and around it like a corkscrew ran a runway that went to the top. There at the top were altars on which were offered human sacrifices. The Babylonians had a postal system second to none. They had interior bathtubs with brass plumbing. They were a literate people with a tremendous library there in the city. Around the city was a three hundred foot high wall, wide enough that four chariots could ride abreast upon it, and which well protected the entire city.

While the head of gold on the multimetallic image represents the outward glory of this advanced civilization, the cruel nature of the lion describes the brutal paganism of this kingdom, which is clearly illustrated in chapters 2 and 3 of the Book of Daniel.

> **And behold another beast, a second, like to a bear, and it raised up itself on one side, and it had three ribs in the mouth of it between the teeth of it: and they said thus unto it, Arise, devour much flesh [Dan. 7:5].**

The bear, representing the kingdom of Medo-Persia, corresponds to the arms of silver of Nebuchadnezzar's image. As the bear raised itself up on one side, the image was ambidextrous. First he struck with the strong left hand of Medes, conquering Babylon; then he followed through with the right uppercut of the Persians, who took over Egypt and the rest of the world, which had been ruled by Babylon.

"Three ribs in the mouth" are the three kingdoms that constituted this empire: Babylon, Lydia, and Egypt.

There are no wings on this bear, but it was told, "Arise, devour much flesh." The army of the Medo-Persians moved like a great, lumbering, and rumbling bear—they even took their families along with them. It was Xerxes who led about 300,000 men and three hundred ships against Greece at Thermopylae and was defeated. His fleet was destroyed by a storm because God did not intend the East to control the West at that particular time.

> After this I beheld, and lo another, like a leopard, which had upon the back of it four wings of a fowl; the beast had also four heads; and dominion was given to it [Dan. 7:6].

"Leopard" would perhaps be better translated "panther." A panther, which leaps with suddenness upon its helpless prey, represents the Graeco-Macedonian empire of Alexander the Great.

"Four wings" further accentuates the ability of Alexander to move his army with rapidity and to strike suddenly. In comparison it would have made Nebuchadnezzar's army look like it was on a slow train through Arkansas. Strong nations which have gained world dominion have developed the ability to move and strike with great speed. Today, in the cold war, we are witnessing a missiles race as a further refinement of the process of adding more "wings" to a nation.

The "four heads" depict the division of Alexander's empire at the time of his death in his early thirties. Babylon went down in a drunken orgy and so did Alexander—they both went the same way. Our nation is going down the same path today. We are living in a day when the social drink is accepted. Our people don't want their young people on drugs, but they don't mind if they go out drinking. Following the death of Alexander, four of his generals divided the world empire which he had carved out, because each of them knew they could not control the whole. Cassander took Macedonia; Lysimachus took Asia Minor; Seleucus took Syria (out of which came the "little horn" of Daniel 8, Antiochus Epiphanes, who wrought such havoc with the temple in Jerusalem); and finally, Ptolemy took Egypt, and of course, Cleopatra came along later in that line.

Scripture does not give us a historical record of the Graeco-Macedonian kingdom. It falls chronologically between the Old and New Testaments—the period known as the intertestament period. It was, however, the time when the remnant in Palestine endured the greatest suffering at the hands of Egypt and Syria.

> **After this I saw in the night visions, and behold a fourth beast, dreadful and terrible, and strong exceedingly; and it had great iron teeth: it devoured and brake in pieces, and stamped the residue with the feet of it: and it was diverse from all the beasts that were before it; and it had ten horns [Dan. 7:7].**

This nondescript beast with ten horns represents the Roman Empire, just as the legs of iron of Nebuchadnezzar's image did. We will find this interpreted in detail in verses 19–28. We want to get the explanation that the Spirit of God has given to us, and that will deliver us from any speculation.

More attention is given to the fourth beast than to all of the other three put together. This section is very important to us because we are living in the time of the fourth beast—the time when the ten toes and horns are beginning to manifest themselves.

The fourth beast is altogether different from the others, and he is given in a separate vision. All the other beasts have counterparts in the jungles and zoos today. We all have seen a lion, or a bear, or a panther, but we have never seen a beast like this on land or sea or in the air. This is really an unusual beast. After you have had a night of dreaming about beasts like this, I don't think an aspirin tablet or a sleeping pill would do you any good at all! I think you would be awake the rest of the night.

The beast is described as "dreadful and terrible, and strong exceedingly." This beast which represents the Roman Empire is characterized by strength. It incited dread and terror, and it bore no resemblance to any beast that preceded it.

"It had great iron teeth," and this identifies it with the legs of iron of the image vision—which is the Roman Empire. The iron heel of Rome was on the neck of this world for one millennium. A great deal has been said about the Roman Empire, and even to this day it amazes historians. Gibbon has said of it: "The empire of the Romans filled the world, and when the empire fell into the hands of a single person, the world became a safe and dreary prison for his enemies. To resist was fatal and it was impossible to fly."

Another writer, Dr. Robert D. Culver, who has a very fine book on Daniel entitled *Daniel: Decoder of Dreams*, has made this statement: "Two millennia ago, Rome gave the world the ecumenical unity which the League of Nations and the United Nations organizations have sought to give in our time. The modern attempts are not original at all (as many of our contemporaries suppose), but are revivals of the ancient Roman ideal which never since the time of Augustus Caesar has been wholly lost."

The Roman Empire simply fell apart; it lives on in many nations of Europe, in those nations which border the Mediterranean and in North Africa—all those which were a part of the Roman Empire. No one overcame Rome, but it fell apart into these different nations.

This unusual beast had ten horns, which obviously correspond to the feet of the image with ten toes. The emphasis is not upon the origin of this empire, but rather upon the *end time*—the period of the ten horns.

The vision of this fourth beast is made even more important to us because it is yet unfulfilled. Apparently we are living in some period toward the end of time. The visions of the three beasts have been fulfilled, which means that three-fourths of this prophecy has already been literally fulfilled; there remains for the future only the time of the "horns." The fourth kingdom of Rome has already appeared. Although it fell apart, it will come back together in ten kingdoms. It will be put together by the one whom the Word of God has labeled the Antichrist.

> I consider the horns, and behold, there came up among them another little horn, before whom there were three of the first horns plucked up by the roots: and, behold, in this horn were eyes like the eyes of man, and a mouth speaking great things [Dan. 7:8].

Our attention is now directed to the ten horns. Notice that they do not represent a fifth kingdom: they grow out of the head of the fourth beast and are the last development of the fourth beast. In the toes of the first vision, the vision of the image, they are iron and clay. Iron is still there—Rome is still there, but the clay, the weakness, is there also. I think the iron represents the autocratic rule of one man, and the clay represents the crowd, a democracy.

Very candidly, we see that type of weakness in democracy today. We are proud of the freedom we have—I thank God we have it—but it is almost a joke to talk about how important John Q. Public is. You and I are not very important, to tell the truth. Oh, every now and then when it's time for elections, the politicians tell us how important and wonderful and educated we are. However, we have very little to do with the control of our government or with the choice of our president. The lobbyists and the politicians are making the choices. I thank God for the liberty we have, but we have been brainwashed to think as they think.

God's ideal government is not a democracy—it is a real dictatorship. When Jesus Christ rules on this earth, He is not going to ask anyone what he wants done. He is going to make the choices, and this earth is going to be run the way He wants to run it. That is the reason it would be best if you and I would become conformed to His image; otherwise we will be very uncomfortable under His dictatorship. Actually, He will put out of His Kingdom anything that offends, anyone who is in rebellion against Him. We are to bow to Him and to His absolute rule.

Rome fell apart because of internal corruption and rottenness and drunkenness. All four of these empires went down with drunkenness. In our own country we say drugs are a problem, but liquor is legal. Who are we kidding? My friend, there are millions of alcoholics trying to hold down jobs today. That is only part of the problem, because that does not include the number of housewives and even children who are alcoholics but are not represented in the statistics. No one knows about them until they commit suicide or need to be put into a mental institution. That is the picture of America in the dark hour in which we live.

Rome is going to be put together again, and it is interesting that men are looking for someone who will be able to do it. The German historian Hoffman has said this: "When Germans and Slavs advanced partly into Roman ground, anyhow into the historical position of the

Roman Empire, their princes intermarried with Roman families. Charlemagne was descended from a Roman house; almost at the same time the German Emperor Otho II and the Russian Grand-Prince Vladimir intermarried with daughters of the East-Roman Emperor. This was characteristic for the relation of the immigrating nations to Rome; *they did not found a new kingdom, but continued the Roman.* And so it continues to the end of all earthly power, until its final ramification into ten kingdoms. To attempt now to mark out these would be as misplaced as to fix the Coming of Christ (with which they stand connected) tomorrow or the next day."

"Another little horn" becomes the key to the entire situation. He uproots three of the ten horns and establishes himself over all. I do not know who the ten kingdoms are, but they come from the disintegration of the Roman Empire.

"In this horn were eyes," denoting human intelligence and genius.

"A mouth speaking great things" denotes the blasphemy of this man.

THE VISIONS OF THE SON OF MAN COMING IN CLOUDS OF HEAVEN

I beheld till the thrones were cast down, and the Ancient of days did sit, whose garment was white as snow, and the hair of his head like the pure wool: his throne was like the fiery flame, and his wheel as burning fire [Dan. 7:9].

The scene shifts to heaven, and the throne of God is revealed. This is the same scene described in chapters 4 and 5 of the Book of Revelation. It is the preparation for the judgment of the Great Tribulation and the second coming of Christ to the earth.

"I beheld till the thrones were cast down [placed]" corresponds to Revelation 4:4. While in revelation John gives the number of the elders and other details, Daniel is not concerned with such since his subject does not include the church and its future.

"The Ancient of days" is the eternal God.

"Whose garment was white as snow" refers to His attributes of holiness and righteousness.

"The hair of his head like the pure wool" speaks of His infinite
wisdom.

"His throne was like the fiery flame" speaks of judgment (see Rev.
4:5).

"His wheels as burning fire" speaks of the resistless energy and
restless power of God (cf. Ezek. 1:13–21).

> **A fiery stream issued and came forth from before him:
> thousand thousands ministered unto him, and ten thou-
> sand times ten thousand stood before him: the judgment
> was set, and the books were opened [Dan. 7:10].**

This is not the Great White Throne judgment which occurs after the
Millennium, but is the setting for the judgment of the Great Tribulation and the return of Christ to establish His millennial Kingdom here
upon earth (see Rev. 5:11–14).

> **I beheld then because of the voice of the great words
> which the horn spake: I beheld even till the beast was
> slain, and his body destroyed, and given to the burning
> flame [Dan. 7:11].**

While God is setting the judgment scene in heaven to determine who
will enter the Kingdom, on earth "the little horn" is blaspheming and
boasting the loudest (see Rev. 13:5–6). However, his judgment is fixed
and his kingdom is doomed.

The emphasis with this kingdom, represented by the last beast, is
not on its beginning but on its end. The appearance of "the little
horn" is shortly before Christ comes to judge living nations and individuals. This period is the Great Tribulation period.

> **As concerning the rest of the beasts, they had their do-
> minion taken away: yet their lives were prolonged for a
> season and time [Dan. 7:12].**

Although the first three beasts were destroyed, the ideology and philosophy of the kingdoms they represent apparently live on and will be manifested in the Great Tribulation period.

I saw in the night visions, and, behold, one like the Son of man came with the clouds of heaven, and came to the Ancient of days, and they brought him near before him [Dan. 7:13].

The Son of God in heaven is here invested with the authority to take the kingdoms of this world from the Gentiles and establish His Kingdom. Jesus referred to this passage when He was put on oath at His trial before the Sanhedrin: ". . . Again the high priest asked him, and said unto him, Art thou the Christ, the Son of the Blessed? And Jesus said, I am: and ye shall see the Son of man sitting on the right hand of power, and coming in the clouds of heaven" (Mark 14:61–62). The angel prophesied at the time of His birth: "He shall be great, and shall be called the Son of the Highest: and the Lord God shall give unto him the throne of his father David" (Luke 1:32).

Therefore what we have here is a very clear-cut statement that the Lord Jesus is that "stone cut out without hands" which smites the image—He will establish His Kingdom here upon earth. In the second Psalm we read: "I will declare the decree: the LORD hath said unto me, Thou art my Son; this day have I begotten thee" (Ps. 2:7). He was begotten from the dead—this refers to His resurrection, not to His birth in Bethlehem. The apostle Paul gives us this interpretation in Acts 13:33. The psalmist goes on to say: "Ask of me, and I shall give thee the heathen for thine inheritance, and the uttermost parts of the earth for thy possession" (Ps. 2:8). Jesus Christ is going to take over the kingdom. How will He do it?—"Thou shalt break them with a rod of iron; thou shalt dash them in pieces like a potter's vessel" (Ps. 2:9). When He comes to the earth, the Millenium will not be there waiting for Him. He will put out all rebellion, and those who are obedient will enter into the Kingdom.

And there was given him dominion, and glory, and a kingdom, that all people, nations, and languages,

**should serve him: his dominion is an everlasting domin-
ion, which shall not pass away, and his kingdom that
which shall not be destroyed [Dan. 7:14].**

This prepares the way for the coming of Christ and the smashing of
the image by the "stone cut out without hands" (see Rev. 19:11–16).

"An everlasting dominion" seems to contradict the idea of a millennial Kingdom of one thousand years. However, at the end of the
thousand years, which is a test period with Christ ruling, there will be
a brief moment of rebellion against Him when Satan is released for a
brief season, and then the Kingdom will go right on into eternity.

Revelation 20:6 says, "Blessed and holy is he that hath part in the
first resurrection: on such the second death hath no power, but they
shall be priests of God and of Christ, and shall reign with him a thousand years." The thousand-year Kingdom is but a phase of the everlasting Kingdom. The steps are outlined clearly in Revelation 20:
Christ reigns a thousand years on the earth under heavenly conditions. After this period, Satan is released. The unregenerate human
heart, still in rebellion against God, rallies to Satan's leadership, and
he assembles them to make war against Christ. Satan and the rebel-
lious betrayers are cast into the lake of fire. The lost dead are raised for
judgment before the Great White Throne. After this, the eternal aspect
of the Kingdom comes into purview (see v. 27).

The Word of God makes it very clear that the location of this Kingdom is on the earth. In Micah 4:2 we read: "And many nations shall
come, and say, Come, and let us go up to the mountain of the LORD,
and to the house of the God of Jacob; and he will teach us of his ways,
and we will walk in his paths: for the law shall go forth of Zion, and
the word of the LORD from Jerusalem."

THE DEFINITION OF THE FOUR BEASTS

**I Daniel was grieved in my spirit in the midst of my
body, and the visions of my head troubled me.**

I came near unto one of them that stood by, and asked
him the truth of all this. So he told me, and made me
know the interpretation of the things [Dan. 7:15–16].

As the dream of the image troubled Nebuchadnezzar, this vision dis-
turbs Daniel. He approaches one of the heavenly creatures for an explanation.

These great beasts, which are four, are four kings,
which shall arise out of the earth [Dan. 7:17].

These four beasts are not only kingdoms but kings. Nebuchadnezzar,
together with his kingdom of Babylon, was represented by the head of
gold and the two-winged lion. Alexander the Great, synonymous with
the Graeco-Macedonian Empire, is depicted by both the sides of brass
and a panther. These wild beasts of prey, with their carnivorous and
voracious natures, are representative of the character of both the king
and the kingdom.

But the saints of the most High shall take the kingdom,
and possess the kingdom for ever, even for ever and ever
[Dan. 7:18].

The identity of "the saints" is the important factor of this statement.
There are five verses in this chapter which mention them (see also
vv. 21–22, 25, 27). Reference to them occurs again in Daniel 8:24.
Immediately one school of prophetic interpretation assumes they are
New Testament saints. A great many people think even narrower than
that; they feel that their denomination or their little group is the
saints. My friend, God has a pretty big family. In the Old Testament He
had Old Testament saints. The nation Israel was called saints; the
Gentiles who came in as proselytes were called saints of God. That's a
different company from New Testament saints today who are in the
church. Don't get the idea that your little group is the only group that
will be saved or even the idea that believers in this dispensation of

grace are the only ones to be saved. God saved people before the Day of Pentecost, and He is going to be saving people after the Rapture. God is in the saving business; maybe the church is failing to reach people with the gospel as it should be, but God is not failing at all.

Daniel 8:24 says, "His power shall be mighty, but not by force of arms; in astonishing ways he shall bring ruin. He shall succeed in what he undertakes. He shall destroy mighty opponents; also the holy people." The "holy people" are the saints. Exodus 19:6 identifies Israel as the holy nation or saints: "And ye shall be unto me a kingdom of priests, and an holy nation . . . ."

The Greek word for "saints" is *hagios*, and it occurs two hundred times in the New Testament. Ninety-two times *hagios* is translated "holy" in combination with "spirit," for the Holy Spirit. It is also used to speak of believers in the church who are called "saints" or "holy ones." In the New Testament, "saints" are the sinners who have been declared righteous because of their faith in Christ (see Rom. 1:7). *Hagios* is used likewise for Old Testament believers (see Matt. 27:52–53) and for tribulation saints (see Rev. 13:7). In the Book of Daniel, therefore, "the saints" refer to people of Israel—not to all Israel but to the believing remnant only. That the church saints are not in view here is evident since Daniel does not refer to the church in any sense.

THE EXPLANATION OF THE FOURTH BEAST

The emphasis is placed on the fourth beast. Here is where Daniel put the emphasis and where God put the emphasis. We ought to also, as our period in history fits somewhere in the time of the fourth beast.

> **Then I would know the truth of the fourth beast, which was diverse from all the others, exceeding dreadful, whose teeth were of iron, and his nails of brass; which devoured, brake in pieces, and stamped the residue with his feet;**
>
> **And of the ten horns that were in his head, and of the other which came up, and before whom three fell; even**

of that horn that had eyes, and a mouth that spake very great things, whose look was more stout than his fellows [Dan. 7:19–20].

Everything here speaks of power and fierceness. The ferocity of the beast, with its iron teeth and brass nails, is noted again. Rome was hated by her captive nations. Hannibal vowed vengeance against her cruel power and lived to execute it; yet he was finally subdued by Rome. Rome rejected the Son of God, the Savior, through her puppet Pilate, who asked the cynical and contemptuous question of Jesus, "What is truth?" Rome crucified Jesus and persecuted the church.

The ten horns grow out of the beast, denoting a later development, not a separate kingdom. Note that the horns do not grow out of a dead beast. Rome *lives* in the fragmentation of the empire in the many existing nations of Europe and North Africa, including perhaps some of Asia. However, I do not think we can specifically identify the nations.

At the time of the end, three of the horns will fall before "the little horn" who is dominant in personality, ability, propaganda, and public appeal. "The little horn" is Antichrist, the Man of Sin (2 Thess. 2:3–4), and the first Beast (Rev. 13:3–6).

I beheld, and the same horn made war with the saints, and prevailed against them [Dan. 7:21].

It should be noted that Rome will again be a world power under Antichrist. We are told in Revelation 13:7—"And it was given unto him to make war with the saints, and to overcome them: and power was given him over all kindreds, and tongues, and nations." This will be a brief period in the last part of the Great Tribulation (see Rev. 11:3; 12:6; 13:5). The church will be removed before the Tribulation begins.

The Romans have been a warlike people. Our ancestors in Europe have been warlike people for fifteen hundred years, and we still are. You cannot go into any city or small town in this country today without seeing a monument to our war dead. G. K. Chesterton said, "One of the paradoxes of this age is that it is the age of pacifism, but not the age of peace." Oh, people carry placards about peace, but we are not a peaceful people. The Bible says, "For when they shall say, Peace and safety; then sudden destruction cometh upon them, as travail upon a woman with child; and they shall not escape" (1 Thess. 5:3). War is in our hearts. In recorded history man has engaged in fifteen thousand wars and has signed some eight thousand peace treaties; yet in all that time, he has enjoyed only two to three hundred years of true peace. Man is a warlike creature.

The Roman Empire is to be put together again, and the Antichrist will be the one to do it. He will march to world power and will become the world ruler. We are told he will blaspheme the God of heaven: "And he opened his mouth in blasphemy against God, to blaspheme his name, and his tabernacle, and them that dwell in heaven" (Rev. 13:6).

What is the picture in Europe today? Early in the 1950s a University of Oklahoma professor traveled through Europe, and although it was less than a decade since the close of World War II with all of its death and destruction, he reported that there was ample evidence the people were looking for a strong man, a leader like Hitler or Napoleon, who would restore their nations to the grandeur and glory and prosperity they once knew.

Even a man like Bishop Fulton J. Sheen made this statement: "The Antichrist will come disguised as the great humanitarian. He will talk peace, prosperity, and plenty, not as a means to lead us to God but as ends in themselves. He will explain guilt away psychologically and make men shrink in shame if their fellowmen say they are not broadminded and liberal. He will spread the lie that men will never be better until they make society better."

My friend, the world is moving toward the time when Europe will come together. I don't know how far away it is. The Common Market is evidence that Europe is moving in that direction; yet it does not mean that we have come to the end.

Another thing has happened in Europe that provides the psychological basis for its coming together. The young people of Italy, France, and Germany, for instance, do not want to be called Italians, French, and Germans. They like to be called Europeans. What a preparation for the coming of Antichrist! Europe today is like ripe fruit hanging on a tree—all the Antichrist needs to do is come and pick it. However, he is not going to come until the Lord removes the church from the world as we read in 1 and 2 Thessalonians.

> **Until the Ancient of days came, and judgment was given to the saints of the most High; and the time came that the saints possessed the kingdom [Dan. 7:22].**

"The Ancient of days" is Christ; He is the only One Who is going to be able to put down Antichrist.

"The saints." Again, we are not talking about New Testament saints—this is the Old Testament. Let the Bible say what it wants to say and don't try to make it fit your little jigsaw puzzle of doctrine.

> **Thus he said, The fourth beast shall be the fourth kingdom upon earth, which shall be diverse from all kingdoms, and shall devour the whole earth, and shall tread it down, and break it in pieces [Dan. 7:23].**

The fourth beast is identified here as a kingdom and in verse 17 as a king. It is impossible to separate the king from his kingdom; both belong together like two sides of a door.

> **And the ten horns out of this kingdom are ten kings that shall arise: and another shall rise after them; and he shall be diverse from the first, and he shall subdue three kings [Dan. 7:24].**

There are ten horns that come out of this fourth beast, and they denote the final form of the fourth kingdom. Each of these kings represents a kingdom. An eleventh king, "the little horn," will arise. He is going to be diverse from the others and will move to world power by subduing three of the kings. He will actually become the dictator of the entire world. This is the picture that is given to us in Revelation 13:7—"And it was given unto him to make war with the saints, and to overcome them: and power was given him over all kindreds, and tongues, and nations." He is the Man of Sin, the Antichrist, and he is going to rule the world during the Great Tribulation period, which is a period of seven years.

And he shall speak great words against the most High, and shall wear out the saints of the most High, and think to change times and laws: and they shall be given into his hand until a time and times and the dividing of time [Dan. 7:25].

The little horn is a blasphemer. "And there was given unto him a mouth speaking great things and blasphemies; and power was given unto him to continue forty and two months. And he opened his mouth in blasphemy against God, to blaspheme his name, and his tabernacle, and them that dwell in heaven" (Rev. 13:5-6).

One of the characteristics of Antichrist is that he is against God and *against Christ*. That is one of the meanings of "antichrist"; the other meaning is to *imitate Christ*. I believe that the two beasts of Revelation 13 represent these two aspects of Antichrist: (1) that he is against Christ and a blasphemer; and (2) that he is a false prophet and attempts to imitate Christ; although he acts like a lamb, he really is a wolf in sheep's clothing.

We are also told that he "shall wear out the saints of the most High." That doesn't mean like some of us preachers wear out the saints on Sunday mornings! It means literally to afflict and persecute the saints (see Rev. 12:13-17).

"And think to change times and laws"—the little horn will change customs and laws.

The period of the little horn's reign is of short duration: "they shall be given into his hand until a time and times and the dividing of time."

"Time"	1 year
"Times"	2 years
"Dividing of time"	½ year
	3½ years

It is during the last three and one-half years of the Great Tribulation that he will reign over the earth (see Rev. 11:2–3; 12:6; 13:5).

> **But the judgment shall sit, and they shall take away his dominion, to consume and to destroy it unto the end [Dan. 7:26].**

"The judgment shall sit" reminds us of the scene in heaven in Revelation 4 and 5 where thrones are depicted. It is determined by the One on the central throne and by the Lamb who is the executor of the judgment, and it is the agreement of all God's created and redeemed intelligences of heaven that the beast must be put down. His dominion must be ended and he himself judged. "The judgment shall sit"— this cannot be changed. This judgment continues through the Great Tribulation and is consummated by the return of Christ to the earth to establish His Kingdom (see Rev. 19:11–21). Thus will end "the times of the Gentiles" which began with Nebuchadnezzar and will continue until the return of Christ.

> **And the kingdom and dominion, and the greatness of the kingdom under the whole heaven, shall be given to the people of the saints of the most High, whose kingdom is an everlasting kingdom, and all dominions shall serve and obey him [Dan. 7:27].**

This is a reference to the eternal Kingdom which appears first in its millennial aspect (see Rev. 20) and then opens up into eternity. Those who find fault with the premillennial position say that the Millennium is not an accurate interpretation but that the Kingdom is an *eternal* Kingdom. However, the Millennium is simply a thousand-year period of testing such as we are in today, and it leads and eventuates into the eternal Kingdom.

This is the statement of Irenaeus, one of the early church fathers: "But then this Antichrist shall have devastated all things in this world, he will reign for three years and six months, and sit in the temple at Jerusalem; and then the Lord will come from heaven in the clouds, in the glory of the Father, sending this man and those who follow him into the lake of fire; but bringing in for the righteous the times of the kingdom, that is, the rest, the hallowed seventh day; and restoring to Abraham the promised inheritance in which kingdom the Lord declared that 'Many coming from the east and from the west should sit down with Abraham, Isaac, and Jacob. . . .'" It is wearisome to hear men try to dissipate and dissolve the Millennium and God's dispensational program for this world by saying that the early church fathers were not premillennial.

Note also this statement by the historian, Philip Schaff: "The most striking point in the eschatology of the ante-Nicene age is the prominent chiliasm, or millenarianism, that is their belief of a visible reign of Christ in glory on earth with the risen saints for a thousand years, before the general resurrection and judgment. It was indeed not the doctrine of the church embodied in any creed or form of devotion, but a widely current opinion of distinguished teachers." May I say to you, you are in good company today if you believe we are going to have a Millennium here on earth.

> **Hitherto is the end of the matter. As for me Daniel, my cogitations much troubled me, and my countenance changed in me: but I kept the matter in my heart [Dan. 7:28].**

Daniel did not divulge to his contemporaries the visions and their contents since they belonged to the end time. They were disturbing to Daniel, however, and made such an impression upon him as to alter his entire outlook. This was something brand new to him.

The study of prophecy in this day is not for the selfish gratification of idle curiosity or vain knowledge. Rather, the careful, prayerful study of prophetic Scripture has a transforming effect upon the life of a believer.

CHAPTER 8

Vision
microscopal
the to
Persian — Greece
Chap. 7

THEME: *Daniel's vision of the ram and he goat; the meaning of the vision*

The vision recorded by Daniel in this chapter was prophetic when it was given, but it has since been fulfilled. Because it has been so clearly and literally fulfilled, this chapter is the basis for the liberal critic giving a late date for the writing of the Book of Daniel. His argument rests on the fact that prophecy concerning the future is supernatural and he does not believe in the supernatural; therefore, this prophecy could not have been written at the time of Daniel, but must have been written afterward as history. That is a very weak argument, and I won't say anymore than that the Book of Daniel was written by the prophet Daniel. You know, there is a debate among some scholars as to whether Shakespeare wrote Shakespeare. Mark Twain's amusing reply to that question was that if Shakespeare didn't write Shakespeare, it must have been written by another man of the same name! Well, if Daniel did not write the Book of Daniel at about 600 B.C., then it must have been written by another man of the same name at the same date.

Daniel's prophetic vision of the ram with two unmatched horns and the he goat with one horn places a microscope down on the conflict between the second and third world empires and the struggle between the East and the West, between the Orient and Occident, between Asia and Europe. This was the struggle between the Medo-Persian and the Graeco-Macedonian empires. The vision includes another "little horn," who has already been fulfilled in Antiochus Epiphanes, the great persecutor of the Jews called "the Nero of Jewish history."

We should also note that the preceding section (see Dan. 2:4—7:28) was written in Aramaic, the original language of Syria and the world language of these four great empires. With the beginning of chapter 8, the book returns to the use of the Hebrew language.

THE VISION OF THE RAM AND HE GOAT

In the third year of the reign of king Belshazzar a vision appeared unto me, even unto me Daniel, after that which appeared unto me at the first [Dan. 8:1].

This is the third year of the reign of Belshazzar, the last king of Babylon. The vision given in chapter 7 was in the first year of his reign; therefore, both of these visions took place toward the end of the Babylonian empire.

And I saw in a vision; and it came to pass, when I saw, that I was at Shushan in the palace, which is in the province of Elam; and I saw in a vision, and I was by the river of Ulai [Dan. 8:2].

In the vision Daniel finds himself at Shushan, which is Susa, the capital of Medo-Persia, the second world empire.

"In the palace" is more accurately, "near the fortress."

"Ulai" is the Kerkah River which flowed by Susa.

The reason for the setting of the vision being at Susa rather than at Babylon is that this vision concerns the second and third world empires. The events foretold in this vision were all fulfilled within two hundred years. Such fulfillment is so remarkable that the liberal critic insists upon a late dating of the Book of Daniel. That is, he maintains that Daniel was written *after* these events had transpired and so is merely a historical record. This is an attempt to get rid of the miraculous, which is embarrassing to his system of interpretation.

Then I lifted up mine eyes, and saw, and, behold, there stood before the river a ram which had two horns: and the two horns were high; but one was higher than the other, and the higher came up last [Dan. 8:3].

"A ram which had two horns" will be identified later as Media-Persia (see v. 20).

"The higher came up last." In other words, the horn representing Media came up first when Gobryas the Median general destroyed Babylon. Then later the Persian monarchs gained the ascendency over the Medes and took the great empire to its highest peak. This ram, then, with its two horns and one horn more prominent than the other, is the Medo-Persian Empire with the Persians being in the ascendancy.

> I saw the ram pushing westward, and northward, and southward; so that no beasts might stand before him, neither was there any that could deliver out of his hand; but he did according to his will, and became great [Dan. 8:4].

"I saw the ram pushing westward, and northward, and southward." Why doesn't it say he was pushing eastward? Persia was in the East and made no further advance into the Far East. If they had gone farther in that direction, they would have stepped into the Orient, into India and China. However, they were projecting their empire in all other directions. This is the empire which was represented by the bear in chapter 7; they were motivated by the spirit of conquest.

> And as I was considering, behold, an he goat came from the west on the face of the whole earth, and touched not the ground: and the goat had a notable horn between his eyes [Dan. 8:5].

As Daniel was marveling at the power and ability of the ram, yonder from the west came a goat with great movement and a dominant horn. The goat represents Greece (see v. 21), and the horn typifies Alexander the Great.

Under Xerxes, Persia intended to move west, but from the West came this goat which was moving so fast it "touched not the ground"—that corresponds to the four wings of the panther and denotes the speed with which Alexander moved his army.

**And he came to the ram that had two horns, which I had
seen standing before the river, and ran unto him in the
fury of his power.**

**And I saw him come close unto the ram, and he was
moved with choler against him, and smote the ram, and
brake his two horns: and there was no power in the ram
to stand before him, but he cast him down to the ground,
and stamped upon him: and there was none that could
deliver the ram out of his hand [Dan. 8:6–7].**

"He was moved with choler" means that he was moved with anger
and great hatred. He ran into him in order to destroy him.

Xerxes was the last great ruler of Persia, and he made a foray
against Europe, against Greece. He moved with an army of 300,000
men and their families. The Greeks were smart—they didn't go out to
meet him. Instead, they waited until he got to Thermopylae, which
was a narrow pass into which he could not fit a big army. Since one
Greek soldier was equal to at least ten of the Medo-Persians, who were
not a trained and disciplined army as the Greeks were, the Greeks
gained the victory at Thermopylae. They decimated that tremendous
Persian army as it attempted to advance through the pass a few sol-
diers at a time. And then at Salamis, Xerxes' fleet of three hundred
vessels was destroyed by a storm. When word was brought to him that
his fleet had been destroyed, he went down to the sea, took off his
belt, and beat the waves with it—they had destroyed his fleet! I would
say that that was not the action of an outstanding and intelligent man,
by any means.

This marked the last effort of the East to move toward the West; no
great advance was ever made again. It is true that the great hordes of
Mohammed, the Moors, came up through Spain, but Charles Martel
stopped them at the battle of Tours. It is also true that the Turks attempted to come through the East, through the Balkans, but they
failed.

Now there rises in the West this tremendous general, a young man,
Alexander the Great. He was only thirty-two years old when he died.

He was a military genius, one of the greatest. He could move a striking force by land quicker than any man ever had.

> **Therefore the he goat waxed very great: and when he was strong, the great horn was broken; and for it came up four notable ones toward the four winds of heaven [Dan. 8:8].**

"When he was strong, the great horn was broken." What was it that broke this horn? There was no human power that could break it. We are told that when he came to power, the whole world was under the heel of Alexander the Great. Tradition says that he sat down and wept because there were no more worlds to conquer—he had conquered the then-known world. However, in the midst of his vast projects, he was seized by a fever after a nightlong drinking bout, and he died in Babylon in the year 323 B.C. at the age of thirty-two. "When he was strong, the great horn was broken."

All three of these empires—the Babylonian, the Medo-Persian, and the Graeco-Macedonian—went down in a drunken orgy. Let me say that I do not think our nation will be destroyed by marijuana or heroin, but alcohol will destroy it. Don't misunderstand me—I am not for legalizing marijuana, and I believe the drug traffic is a grave danger, but we have lost sight of the fact that alcohol destroys nations.

According to the latest 1981 statistics I have seen, about 26,000 Americans are killed and another million suffer crippling and other serious injuries every year in drunk-driving incidents. We have had protest movements over the deaths caused by war, but do we see anyone carrying a whiskey bottle, saying, "This is the real danger to America today"? The drinking-driver problem creates an estimated economic cost of more than five billion dollars annually. There are no statistics on the unemployed who are alcoholics. Billions of dollars are spent each year for liquor. The facts are alarming.

The great empire of Alexander the Great went down because he was an alcoholic. He conquered the world, but he could not conquer Alexander the Great. There is grave danger in Washington, D.C., today, which is that many decisions of our government are made during cocktail parties. Why do we think we are something special? Why are there people who think that the United States happens to be God's little pet nation? We think we are so superior intellectually, the ultimate product of the evolutionary process, and there is no chance that we will go down as a nation. My friend, it is time someone blew the whistle and announced that we are on the way out. If I read prophecy correctly, we are on the way out.

"And for it came up four notable ones." When Alexander died, his empire was divided among four men (which correspond to the four heads of the panther in ch. 7). These were the four generals who divided the empire: Cassander, who was married to Alexander's sister and took the European section (Macedonia and Greece); Lysimachus who took the great part of Asia Minor, which is modern Turkey; Seleucus who took Asia, all the eastern part of the empire, except Egypt; and Ptolemy who took Egypt and North Africa.

> **And out of one of them came forth a little horn, which waxed exceeding great, toward the south, and toward the east, and toward the pleasant land [Dan. 8:9].**

"The pleasant land" is Israel.

The "little horn" of this chapter is not the same as described in the previous chapter. There the little horn arises out of the fourth kingdom; here the little horn comes out of the third kingdom. This little horn is historical, while the little horn of chapter 7 is to be revealed in the future. The little horn being presently considered came out of Syria from the Seleucid dynasty. He was Antiochus IV, or Epiphanes, the son of Antiochus the Great. He is sometimes called Epiphanes, "the madman"—he was another demented ruler.

Antiochus came to the throne in 175 B.C. and he made an attack on Jerusalem. It was against him that the Maccabees were raised up in Judah. Anti-Semitic to the core, he tried to exterminate the Jews. He placed an image of Jupiter in the Holy Place in the temple in Jerusalem. This was the first "abomination of desolation." He also poured swine broth over all the holy vessels.

> **And it waxed great, even to the host of heaven; and it cast down some of the host and of the stars to the ground, and stamped upon them [Dan. 8:10].**

This statement is admittedly difficult to interpret. I think that the natural interpretation is that Antiochus challenged God and was permitted to capture Jerusalem and the temple. This warfare included the spiritual realm where angels and demons were involved. Some of the feats attributed to Antiochus are astounding; if they are true, demonic power was exhibited.

> **Yea, he magnified himself even to the prince of the host, and by him the daily sacrifice was taken away, and the place of his sanctuary was cast down [Dan. 8:11].**

Antiochus was a devotee of Jupiter of whom he may have thought himself an incarnation. He chose for himself the title *Theos Epiphanes,* meaning "God manifest."

> **And an host was given him against the daily sacrifice by reason of transgression, and it cast down the truth to the ground; and it practised, and prospered [Dan. 8:12].**

It was by the permissive will of God that this little horn practiced and prospered during this period.

> **Then I heard one saint speaking, and another saint said unto that certain saint which spake, How long shall be the vision concerning the daily sacrifice, and the transgression of desolation, to give both the sanctuary and the host to be trodden under foot? [Dan. 8:13].**

Saint is a "holy one" and refers to one of God's created intelligences other than man—what we would call a supernatural creature. (I often wonder what angels call us, by the way.)

The profaning of the temple is called here a "transgression of desolation."

> **And he said unto me, Unto two thousand and three hundred days; then shall the sanctuary be cleansed [Dan. 8:14].**

There has always been a great deal of disagreement as to the interpretation of these twenty-three hundred days. Seventh-Day Adventism grew out of the "great second advent awakening" in which this verse was given the day-year interpretation and the date for Christ's second coming was set for the year 1843. William Miller and his followers, among whom was Ellen G. White, understood "the sanctuary" to be the earth which would be cleansed at His coming. Miller was a sincere but badly mistaken Baptist preacher. The day-year interpretation was a fragile and insecure foundation for any theory of prophecy, and history has demonstrated it to be false.

However, if the twenty-three hundred days are taken as being literal twenty-four-hour days, the period would be between six and seven years, which approximates the time of Antiochus who began to perpetrate his atrocities in about 170 B.C. Finally the Jewish priest, Judas Maccabeus ("the hammer"), drove out the Syrian army, at which time the temple was cleansed and rededicated after its pollution. This cleansing is celebrated in the Feast of Lights. In John 10:22 we read: "And it was at Jerusalem the feast of the dedication [rededication of Lights], and it was winter." This was one of the holy days celebrated at the time of Christ and which is still remembered by the Jews. It is a feast not mentioned in the Old Testament at all, because it was established in the intertestamental period between the Old and New Testaments.

THE MEANING OF THE VISION

> **And it came to pass, when I, even I Daniel, had seen the vision, and sought for the meaning, then, behold, there stood before me as the appearance of a man.**

> And I heard a man's voice between the banks of Ulai,
> which called, and said, Gabriel, make this man to un-
> derstand the vision [Dan. 8:15-16].

Daniel was puzzled by the vision, and he desired to learn the meaning of it. There appeared to him the angel Gabriel. This is the first
time Gabriel is introduced to us in the Bible.

> So he came near where I stood: and when he came, I
> was afraid, and fell upon my face: but he said unto me,
> Understand, O son of man: for at the time of the end
> shall be the vision [Dan. 8:17].

Gabriel, in the explanation that follows, will make it clear that Antiochus Epiphanes is but a picture in miniature of the coming Antichrist.

"For at the time of the end shall be the vision." Notice that it is for
"the time of the end," not the end of time. Nowhere in the Bible are we
told about the end of time. "The time of the end" locates the complete
fulfillment of this prophecy in the period which our Lord Jesus called
the Great Tribulation. The man referred to is the Antichrist, also
called the Man of Sin and the little horn of chapter 7. This prophecy
goes beyond the immediate future and is projected into the distant
future—even in our day it is still future. Antiochus is merely an adumbration of the other "little horn" who will come at the end of the
"times of the Gentiles," which is made abundantly clear by the use of
these eschatological terms.

> Now as he was speaking with me, I was in a deep sleep
> on my face toward the ground: but he touched me, and
> set me upright [Dan. 8:18].

Notice the physical effect of this vision upon Daniel.

> And he said, Behold, I will make thee know what shall
> be in the last end of the indignation: for at the time ap-
> pointed the end shall be [Dan. 8:19].

Again Gabriel moves from the local fulfillment in Antiochus to the end of the Times of the Gentiles.

> **The ram which thou sawest having two horns are the kings of Media and Persia [Dan. 8:20].**

They are clearly identified for us; we do not have to speculate. The ram definitely represents the kings of Media and Persia.

> **And the rough goat is the king of Grecia: and the great horn that is between his eyes is the first king [Dan. 8:21].**

So the "rough goat" is likewise labeled the king of Greece, and the "great horn" is the first king, Alexander the Great.

> **Now that being broken, whereas four stood up for it, four kingdoms shall stand up out of the nation, but not in his power [Dan. 8:22].**

In other words, none of these kings would have the power that Alexander the Great had.

> **And in the latter time of their kingdom, when the transgressors are come to the full, a king of fierce countenance, and understanding dark sentences, shall stand up [Dan. 8:23].**

The "little horn" is Antiochus Epiphanes of the line of the Seleucidae that took Syria. The only adequate explanation of this verse and of the facts of history is that this man was demon possessed. In this respect he is also a picture of the coming Antichrist. The Lord Jesus made reference to him when He said, "For there shall arise false Christs, and false prophets, and shall shew great signs and wonders; insomuch that, if it were possible, they shall deceive the very elect" (Matt. 24:24).

> **And his power shall be mighty, but not by his own power: and he shall destroy wonderfully, and shall prosper, and practise, and shall destroy the mighty and the holy people [Dan. 8:24].**

"The holy people" refers to Israel. The slaughter of these people by Antiochus Epiphanes seems almost unbelievable. He was as bad as Hitler. However, he is merely an adumbration of the Antichrist who is coming, of whom it is said: "And it was given unto him to make war with the saints, and to overcome them: and power was given him over all kindreds, and tongues, and nations" (Rev. 13:7).

> **And through his policy also he shall cause craft to prosper in his hand; and he shall magnify himself in his heart, and by peace shall destroy many: he shall also stand up against the Prince of princes; but he shall be broken without hand [Dan. 8:25].**

Antiochus was but a faint type of this king who is coming. And he will do four things which Antiochus did in pygmy style:

1. "He shall cause craft to prosper in his hand." We are told in Revelation 13:17 that no man will be able to buy or sell save the one who has the mark of the beast. He will control the economy with a vengeance.

2. "He shall magnify himself in his heart." Revelation 13:5 says that he is given a mouth speaking great things and blasphemies. He will be given power to continue forty-two months. Humility is not a characteristic of the Antichrist! He is like Satan who was filled with pride.

3. "By peace shall destroy many." He comes in as a lamb, but he goes out as a lion. In Revelation 6 he is the rider on the white horse. Notice that right after him comes the red horse of *war*—he has brought in a false peace.

4. "He shall stand up against the Prince of princes." You see, he will oppose and fight against Christ. One of the marks of Antichrist and of that first beast in Revelation 13 is that he is against Christ.

**And the vision of the evening and the morning which
was told is true: wherefore shut thou up the vision; for it
shall be for many days [Dan. 8:26].**

Daniel was told that the vision would be for the distant future—"for it
shall be for many days" to come.

**And I Daniel fainted, and was sick certain days; after-
ward I rose up, and did the king's business; and I was
astonished at the vision, but none understood it [Dan.
8:27].**

The physical and psychological effect of this vision upon Daniel was
devastating. At this point God was beginning to mesh the "times of
the Gentiles" into the history of the nation Israel. That was the thing
that puzzled Daniel at the first, and it still puzzles a great many people. How can God mesh His program with Israel into His program for
the Gentiles in the world? And today to further complicate it, there is
His program with the church. The answer is quite simple, of course.
In our day God is calling out a people to His name—we label this
called-out group "the church." When that is concluded, and the
church is removed from the earth at the Rapture, then He will again
turn to His purpose with Israel and the gentile nations.

CHAPTER 9

THEME: The prayer of Daniel; prophecy of the Seventy
Weeks

This is another one of those remarkable chapters in Scripture. Dr.
Philip Newell evaluates it, "The greatest chapter in the book and
one of the greatest chapters of the entire Bible." The double theme is
prayer and prophecy. If one were to choose the ten greatest chapters of
the Bible on the subject of prayer, this chapter would be included on
any list. If the ten most important chapters on prophecy were chosen,
this chapter would again be included on any list. The first 21 verses
give us the prayer of Daniel, and the final 6 verses give us the very
important prophecy of the Seventy Weeks.

THE PRAYER OF DANIEL

This prayer of Daniel is actually a culmination of a life of prayer. Daniel asked for a prayer meeting to learn the dream of Nebuchadnezzar at
the beginning of the book, and he has been a man of prayer all the way
through. The prayer in this chapter gives the pattern of his prayer life
and acquaints us with the conditions of prayer. Here are some of the
basic elements in the prescription of prayer.

Purposeful Planning. Prayer was no haphazard matter with Daniel. He wrote, "And I set my face upon the Lord God, to seek by prayer
and supplications, with fasting, and sackcloth, and ashes" (v. 3).
Prayer was not just a repetition of idle words or the putting together of
pretty phrases with flowery grammar. The Lord Jesus said, "But when
ye pray, use not vain repetitions, as the heathen do; for they think that
they shall be heard for their much speaking" (Matt. 6:7). Such is not
real prayer.

Painful Performance. Daniel prayed with fasting and sackcloth
and ashes. This was not done for outward show but to reveal the sin-
cerity of his heart. One doesn't see many prayer meetings like that
today.

Perfect Plainness. Daniel was candid and straightforward in his confession. He got right down to business with God.

There is the story of a preacher in a Scottish prayer meeting who got up and started one of his long-winded prayers. Finally a dear old lady pulled his coattail and said, "Parson, call Him 'Father' and ask Him for something." We need more plainness in prayer.

Powerful Petition. Daniel received an answer while he was speaking and praying. The angel Gabriel appeared to him to give him some explanation. This man got *answers* to his prayers. "And this is the confidence that we have in him, that, if we ask any thing according to his will, he heareth us" (1 John 5:14).

Personal and Private. Daniel did not call a public prayer meeting; he prayed privately. This prayer of his is of three minutes' duration. Our Lord often prayed privately. His prayer which is recorded in John 17 is also three minutes long. There are many of us who want to call a public prayer meeting when we ought to spend more time in *private* prayer.

Plenary (full) Penetration. Prayer is the only force that has penetrated outer space to the throne of God. Sir Isaac Newton said that he could take up a telescope and look at the nearest star, but he could put down the telescope, get down on his knees and penetrate the outer heavens to the very throne of God.

Prayer for Daniel was a real exercise of soul in spiritual travail. Such prayer is arduous work. It requires effort and endurance and suffering.

In the first year of Darius the son of Ahasuerus, of the seed of the Medes, which was made king over the realm of the Chaldeans [Dan. 9:1].

"First year of Darius . . . of the seed of the Medes." The two significant questions are: Who was Darius and what was the date? Darius the Mede *may* be identified as Cyaxares II of secular history (Dan. 5:31). "Darius" is more an official title, such as king, czar, or emperor, than an actual name. There has been some disagreement as to the exact date. Newell thinks it is 538 B.C.; Culber places it at 536 B.C. I think either date would fit into the background. This man conquered Babylon in 538 B.C.

In the first year of his reign I Daniel understood by books the numbers of the years, whereof the word of the LORD came to Jeremiah the prophet, that he would accomplish seventy years in the desolations of Jerusalem [Dan. 9:2].

This is in the first year of the reign of Darius. Daniel has now seen a new great world empire come into position, and he is wondering about the future and especially the future of his own people. So Daniel turns to a study of the Word of God. He reads the book of the prophet Jeremiah who said that Israel would be in captivity for seventy years. The date is about 537 B.C. in this chapter. Daniel is between eighty-five and ninety years of age. He had been captured back in 606 B.C. when he was about seventeen. That means that the seventy-year period is coming to a close. It is about the time that these people will be given the opportunity to return to their own land.

Daniel was concerned about his people. I think he was shaken by that little horn in chapter 8, Antiochus Epiphanes, the Syrian king of the Seleucid dynasty. He would abuse Daniel's people, and he would desecrate the temple. All of this caused Daniel great concern.

We should notice that the determining factor which brought Daniel to this prayer was his study of the Word of God. The Word reveals the will of God. A study of God's Word, followed by prayer, is the formula for determining God's will. These are the promises which Daniel read: "And this whole land shall be a desolation, and an astonishment; and these nations shall serve the king of Babylon seventy years" (Jer. 25:11). "For thus saith the LORD, That after seventy years be accomplished at Babylon I will visit you, and perform my good word toward you, in causing you to return to this place" (Jer. 29:10).

Keep in mind that Daniel had been studying Jeremiah's prophecy about these seventy years. When Gabriel used the expression, "seventy weeks" (v. 24), he was extending the time of the seventy years. The Seventy Weeks will cover the entire time of the nation Israel in this time of testing before the Kingdom is established on earth.

Just reading Daniel's prayer reveals how different prayer was in his day from what it is now. Notice first the conditions—

> **And I set my face upon the Lord God, to seek by prayer and supplications, with fasting, and sackcloth, and ashes:**
>
> **And I prayed unto the LORD my God, and made my confession, and said, O Lord, the great and dreadful God, keeping the covenant and mercy to them that love him, and to them that keep his commandments [Dan. 9:3–4].**

"To seek by prayer and supplications, with fasting." We are told that the Lord Jesus fasted, but fasting was never given to the people of God as a service. It was something that one could do over and above what was required. It is mentioned that in the early church there were many who fasted. Paul wrote to the Christians at Corinth: "In weariness and painfulness, in watchings often, in hunger and thirst, in fastings often, in cold and nakedness" (2 Cor. 11:27).

Daniel demonstrated a purposeful persistence in prayer. Even Jacob in his prayer cried, ". . . I will not let thee go, except thou bless me" (Gen. 32:26).

This prayer of Daniel is very personal. It concerns him and his people, which is evident by the repeated use of the first person pronouns, *I, we*, and *our*. They appear forty-one times in this prayer. You may remember that we pointed out how Nebuchadnezzar used the personal pronoun in chapter 4. What is the difference? For Nebuchadnezzar it was a mark of pride, a mark of being lifted up. The contrast of Daniel's use of the personal pronoun is striking. It denotes humility, confession, and "confusion of faces" in contrast to Nebuchadnezzar's pride and self-adulation.

Daniel is down on his face before God. He recognizes the attributes of God. First we see that he rests upon his personal relationship to God. He calls Him, "My God," appealing to God in a very personal way. Before he makes his confession, he dwells on the greatness of God. "Dreadful God" actually means worthy of reverence. One cannot trifle with God.

Daniel acknowledges that God keeps the covenant and mercy to them that love Him. He not only makes promises, but He keeps them. He is immutable and, therefore, He is faithful. He is also a God of mercy. It was by His mercy that the nation Israel had been preserved. It is by His mercy that you and I have been brought to this present moment. It is by His mercy that He saves us. "It is of the LORD's mercies that we are not consumed, because his compassions fail not" (Lam. 3:22). God is gracious, but God also expects us to mean business, and God expects to be obeyed.

Now notice Daniel's confession of sin—

> We have sinned, and have committed iniquity, and have done wickedly, and have rebelled, even by departing from thy precepts and from thy judgments:

> Neither have we hearkened unto thy servants the prophets, which spake in thy name to our kings, our princes, and our fathers, and to all the people of the land [Dan. 9:5-6].

"We have sinned." Daniel identifies himself with his people back there in the land of Israel when they rebelled against God, which resulted in their captivity. He is specific in his confession. He labels each sin: iniquity, wickedness, rebellion, disobedience, and refusal to hear God's prophets. He writes them all down. He doesn't leave any out.

My friend, I believe that our confession of sin requires exactly that. It isn't enough to go to God and say, "I have sinned." Confession means to tell God exactly what we have done. When my wife sends me to the grocery store, she doesn't say, "Get some groceries." She always gives me a list of items. I am to get this, get that, and get the other thing—and four or five more things. I have to go through that list. And I feel that confession of sins should be that specific. Spell it out to Him. Maybe we don't like to do that because it is an ugly thing. But spell it out to Him; He already knows how ugly it is. We need to come to Him in frank, open confession.

> O Lord, righteousness belongeth unto thee, but unto us confusion of faces, as at this day; to the men of Judah, and to the inhabitants of Jerusalem, and unto all Israel, that are near, and that are far off, through all the countries whither thou hast driven them, because of their trespass that they have trespassed against thee [Dan. 9:7].

"All Israel, that are near, and that are far off." The people of Israel were scattered, but there were no lost tribes—it is a misnomer to call them that. Some of the tribes were near Daniel there in Babylon and others were far off, but he knew where they were. He didn't say they were lost. But they were scattered "through all the countries whither thou hast driven them, because of their trespass that they have trespassed against thee."

> O Lord, to us belongeth confusion of face, to our kings, to our princes, and to our fathers, because we have sinned against thee.

> To the Lord our God belong mercies and forgiveness, though we have rebelled against him;

> Neither have we obeyed the voice of the Lord our God, to walk in his laws, which he set before us by his servants the prophets.

> Yea, all Israel have transgressed thy law, even by departing, that they might not obey thy voice; therefore the curse is poured upon us, and the oath that is written in

the law of Moses the servant of God, because we have sinned against him.

And he hath confirmed his words, which he spake against us, and against our judges that judged us, by bringing upon us a great evil: for under the whole heaven hath not been done as hath been done upon Jerusalem.

As it is written in the law of Moses, all this evil is come upon us: yet made we not our prayer before the LORD our God, that we might turn from our iniquities, and understand thy truth.

Therefore hath the LORD watched upon the evil, and brought it upon us: for the LORD our God is righteous in all his works which he doeth: for we obeyed not his voice [Dan. 9:8–14].

Up to this point have you noticed how Daniel contrasted God's goodness with Israel's sin? He contrasted His righteousness with their "confusion of face" which was their shame. They were scattered because of their trespass against God. They deserved the punishment they had received. God was righteous in sending them into captivity. God was right; they were wrong. *NO EXCUSES*

Oh, my friend, if you go to God and make excuses for your sin, if you say to Him, "Lord, you know that I am weak and I was in this and that circumstance," you are blaming your sin upon God. You are saying that God made a mistake—He should have taken those things into consideration. He has been too hard on you! My friend, you and I are getting exactly what we deserve. And we need to go to God in confession of our sin. In our day I hear folk implying that God may be wrong in what He is doing. God is not wrong; we are the ones who are wrong.

Daniel's attitude is the proper attitude that each of us should take as we approach our God in prayer. God will not utterly forsake us, but He certainly is not going to move on our behalf until you and I get to

the place where we can claim the mercy of God and stop making excuses for ourselves.

> **And now, O Lord our God, that hast brought thy people
> forth out of the land of Egypt with a mighty hand, and
> hast gotten thee renown, as at this day; we have sinned,
> we have done wickedly.**
>
> **O Lord, according to all thy righteousness, I beseech
> thee, let thine anger and thy fury be turned away from
> thy city Jerusalem, thy holy mountain: because for our
> sins, and for the iniquities of our fathers, Jerusalem and
> thy people are become a reproach to all that are about
> us.**
>
> **Now therefore, O our God, hear the prayer of thy ser-
> vant, and his supplications, and cause thy face to shine
> upon thy sanctuary that is desolate, for the Lord's sake.**
>
> **O my God, incline thine ear, and hear; open thine eyes,
> and behold our desolations, and the city which is called
> by thy name: for we do not present our supplications be-
> fore thee for our righteousnesses but for thy great mer-
> cies [Dan. 9:15–18].**

This is Daniel's petition and plea. He recalls how God led Israel out of
Egypt. God did it because of *His* righteousness, not because of theirs.
He found the explanation for their deliverance in Himself, not in the
people. "And God heard their groaning, and God remembered his
covenant with Abraham, with Isaac, and with Jacob. And God looked
upon the children of Israel, and God had respect unto them" (Exod.
2:24–25). The only thing that made an appeal to God from the people
was their groaning. In other words, God saw their misery, and He remembered His mercy.

Now Daniel asks God to repeat Himself by delivering them again
because of His righteousness. God is righteous when He extends His
mercy to us, because Jesus Christ has fully paid all the penalty for our

sin. "To declare, I say, at this time his righteousness: that he might be just, and the justifier of him which believeth in Jesus" (Rom. 3:26).

Now notice Daniel's impassioned plea—

> **O Lord, hear; O Lord, forgive; O Lord, hearken and do; defer not, for thine own sake, O my God: for thy city and thy people are called by thy name [Dan. 9:19].**

This is the climactic plea of Daniel. He asks God to hear and answer because of who He is and what He has promised. No good thing rests upon Israel. Daniel doesn't plead because he is Daniel. Rather, he associates himself with his people and says, "We have sinned," including himself, you see. God's name is at stake, and Daniel is deeply concerned about the name of God and the glory of God. This is the basis for his plea.

Now we shall see that while Daniel was praying, an answer was on its way.

> **And whiles I was speaking, and praying, and confessing my sin and the sin of my people Israel, and presenting my supplication before the LORD my God for the holy mountain of my God [Dan. 9:20].**

"Whiles I was speaking, and praying, and confessing my sin." Notice Daniel says, "my sin." Daniel confessed that he was a sinner. It is interesting that there is no place in the Bible which mentions any sin that Daniel committed. In fact, when his enemies were trying to find some wrongdoing in his life, they could find nothing—and we may be sure that they left no stone unturned.

Now I have often made the statement that no one has ever been saved by keeping the Ten Commandments. And I have suggested that if anybody knew of someone in the Old Testament who was saved by keeping the Ten Commandments to let me know about it. Well, one night after a service in which I had said that no one in the Old Testament was ever saved by keeping the Ten Commandments, a UCLA student came up to me and said, "I found a man in the Old Testament who didn't sin. It's Daniel." I told him very frankly that he was right. One cannot find a recorded sin which Daniel committed. Then I showed him this verse where Daniel says, "I was speaking, and praying, and confessing my sin." If Daniel had never sinned but *said* that he was confessing his sin, then he would be lying to say he was confessing sin if, in fact, he had never sinned! So Daniel is a sinner, any way you take it. I think the UCLA student was convinced that the Bible is correct when it says, "For *all* have sinned, and come short of the glory of God" (Rom. 3:23, italics mine).

Now if you are wondering what sin Daniel committed, let me say that it is none of your business, and it is none of my business. God did not record it in His Word.

So Daniel was a sinner, and I can still say that no one was ever saved by keeping the Ten Commandments. Daniel was casting himself and his people upon the mercy of God.

"Presenting my supplication before the LORD my God for the holy mountain of my God"—which would be Jerusalem and the Kingdom of God that will be there (see Isa. 2:1–2).

> **Yea, whiles I was speaking in prayer, even the man Gabriel, whom I had seen in the vision at the beginning, being caused to fly swiftly, touched me about the time of the evening oblation [Dan. 9:21].**

"The man Gabriel"—Gabriel was an angel and apparently appeared in human form. The time of his appearance was at the hour of the evening sacrifice at Jerusalem, which would be approximately three o'clock in the afternoon.

PROPHECY OF THE SEVENTY WEEKS

Now here is the prophecy delivered by Gabriel which makes this chapter of such great importance in the study of eschatology.

> And he informed me, and talked with me, and said, O
> Daniel, I am now come forth to give thee skill and un-
> derstanding.
>
> At the beginning of thy supplications the command-
> ment came forth, and I am come to shew thee; for thou
> art greatly beloved: therefore understand the matter,
> and consider the vision [Dan. 9:22-23].

Notice that Daniel gets an immediate answer to his prayer. I heard Dr.
Gaebelein say that it took him three minutes to read Daniel's prayer in
Hebrew. By the time Daniel finished his prayer, the angel Gabriel was
there. So Dr. Gaebelein reasoned and explained with a twinkle in his
eye, "It took Gabriel three minutes to get from heaven to earth." Of
course, if Daniel had his eyes closed while he was praying, it may be
that Gabriel was standing on one foot and then on the other for two
minutes, waiting for Daniel to get finished. The Lord God has promised, "And it shall come to pass, that before they call, I will answer;
and while they are yet speaking, I will hear" (Isa. 65:24).

Note that Daniel was "greatly beloved" in heaven. That is wonderful. The believer in Jesus Christ is seen by God as being in Christ.
According to Ephesians 1:6 we are accepted in the Beloved—so the
believer is loved in heaven because he is in Christ.

> Seventy weeks are determined upon thy people and
> upon thy holy city, to finish the transgression, and to
> make an end of sins, and to make reconciliation for in-
> iquity, and to bring in everlasting righteousness, and to
> seal up the vision and prophecy, and to anoint the most
> Holy [Dan. 9:24].

"Seventy weeks" does not mean weeks of seven days any more than it
means weeks of seven years or seven other periods of time. The Hebrew word for "seven" is shabua, meaning "a unit of measure." It
would be comparable to our word dozen. When it stands alone, it

could be a dozen of anything—a dozen eggs, a dozen bananas. So here, Seventy Weeks means seventy sevens. It could be seventy sevens of anything. It could be units of days or months or years. In the context of this verse it is plain that Daniel has been reading in Jeremiah about years, seventy years. Jeremiah had been preaching and writing that the captivity would be for seventy years. The seventy years of captivity were the specific penalty for violating seventy sabbatic years. That would be seventy sevens, a total of 490 years. In those 490 years, Israel had violated exactly seventy sabbatic years; so they would go into captivity for seventy years. "To fulfil the word of the LORD by the mouth of Jeremiah, until the land had enjoyed her sabbaths: for as long as she lay desolate she kept sabbath, to fulfil threescore and ten years" (2 Chron. 36:21).

1 week = 7 years
70 weeks = 490 years
70 weeks divided into 3 periods:
7 weeks—62 weeks—1 week

Now Daniel was puzzled as to how the end of the seventy years of captivity would fit into the long period of Gentile world dominion which the visions in chapters 7 and 8 had so clearly indicated. He obviously thought that at the end of the seventy years his people would be returned to the land, the promised Messiah would come, and the Kingdom which had been promised to David would be established. How could both be true? It appeared to him, I am sure, to be an irreconcilable situation created by these seemingly contradictory prophecies.

The Seventy Weeks, or the seventy sevens, answer two questions. Israel's kingdom will not come immediately. The seventy sevens must run their course. These seventy sevens fit into the Times of the Gentiles and run concurrently with them. They are broken up to fit into gentile times. The word for determined literally means "cutting off." These seventy sevens are to be cut off, as the following verses will indicate. The seventy sevens for Israel and the Times of the Gentiles will both come to an end at the same time, that is, at the second coming of Christ. This is important to know for the correct understanding of the prophecy.

The Seventy Weeks concern "thy people," meaning the people of Daniel. That would be Israel. And they concern "the holy city," which can be none other than Jerusalem. Six things are to be accomplished in those Seventy Weeks or 490 years. We will see as we progress in our study that sixty-nine of those "weeks" have already passed, and one "week" is yet to be fulfilled.

Here are the six things to be accomplished:

1. "To finish the transgression." This refers to the transgression of Israel. The cross provided the redemption for sin—for the sin of the nation, but not all accepted it. Today the word has gone out to the ends of the earth that there is a redemption for mankind. But in that last "week" we are told that God says, "And I will pour upon the house of David, and upon the inhabitants of Jerusalem, the spirit of grace and of supplications . . ." (Zech. 12:10). And in Zechariah 13:1: "In that day there shall be a fountain opened to the house of David and to the inhabitants of Jerusalem for sin and for uncleanness." That has not been opened yet. All you have to do is to look at the land of Israel and you will know this has not been fulfilled.

2. "To make an end of sins." The national sins of Israel will come to an end at the second coming of Christ. They are just like any other people or any other nation. They are sinners as individuals and as a nation. They have made many mistakes as a nation (so have we), but God will make an end to that.

3. "To make reconciliation for iniquity." During this period of Seventy Weeks, God has provided a redemption through the death and resurrection of Christ. This, of course, is for Jew and Gentile alike.

4. "And to bring in everlasting righteousness" refers to the return of Christ at the end of the 490 years to establish the Kingdom.

5. "To seal up the vision and prophecy" means that all will be fulfilled, which will vindicate this prophecy as well as all other prophecies in Scripture.

6. "To anoint the most Holy" has reference to the anointing of the Holy of Holies in the millennial temple about which Ezekiel spoke (Ezek. 41—46).

> **Know therefore and understand, that from the going forth of the commandment to restore and to build Jerusalem unto the Messiah the Prince shall be seven weeks, and threescore and two weeks: the street shall be built again, and the wall, even in troublous times.**

> **And after threescore and two weeks shall Messiah be cut off, but not for himself: and the people of the prince that shall come shall destroy the city and the sanctuary; and the end thereof shall be with a flood, and unto the end of the war desolations are determined.**

> **And he shall confirm the covenant with many for one week: and in the midst of the week he shall cause the sacrifice and the oblation to cease, and for the over-**

The 70 WEEKS of DANIEL 9

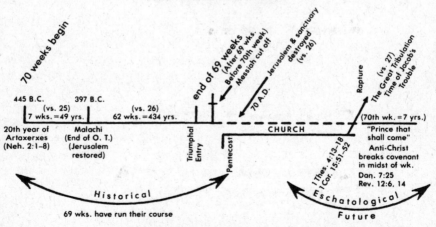

(See Sir Robert Anderson's *The Coming Prince*)

spreading of abominations he shall make it desolate, even until the consummation, and that determined shall be poured upon the desolate [Dan. 9:25-27].

The starting point for this period of 490 years is essential to the correct understanding of the prophecy. Since this period is projected into the Times of the Gentiles, it must fit into secular history and originate from some date connected with the Times of the Gentiles. Of course there have been many suggestions for a starting point: the decree of Cyrus (see Ezra 1:1-4); the decree of Darius (see Ezra 6:1-12); the decree of Artaxerxes—at the seventh year of his reign (Ezra 7:11-26); but I feel that the decree of Artaxerxes in the twentieth year of his reign (Neh. 2:1-8) meets the requirements of verse 25. The commandment to rebuild the city of Jerusalem was issued in the month Nisan 445 B.C. That, then, will be our starting point.

The first seven weeks of forty-nine years bring us to 397 B.C. and to Malachi and the end of the Old Testament. These were "troublous times," as witnessed by both Nehemiah and Malachi.

Sixty-two weeks, or 434 years, bring us to the Messiah. Sir Robert Anderson in his book, *The Coming Prince*, has worked out the time schedule. From the first of the month Nisan to the tenth of Nisan (April 6) A.D. 32, is 173,880 days. Dividing them according to the Jewish year of 360 days, he arrives at 483 years (69 sevens). On this day Jesus rode into Jerusalem, offering Himself for the first time, publicly and officially, as the Messiah.

After the 69 weeks, or 483 years, there is a time break. Between the sixty-ninth and Seventeeth Week two events of utmost importance are to take place:

1. Messiah will be cut off. This was the crucifixion of Christ, the great mystery and truth of the gospel: "From that time forth began Jesus to shew unto his disciples, how that he must go unto Jerusalem, and suffer many things of the elders and chief priests and scribes, and be killed, and be raised again the third day" (Matt. 16:21). "That whosoever believeth in him should not perish, but have eternal life" (John 3:15).

2. Destruction of Jerusalem, which took place in A.D. 70, when Titus the Roman was the instrument.

The final "week" (the seventieth), a period of seven years, is projected into the future and does not follow chronologically the other sixty-nine. The time gap between the sixty-ninth and seventieth weeks is the age of grace—unknown to the prophets (Eph. 3:1–12; 1 Pet. 1:10–12). The Seventieth Week is eschatological; it is the final period and is yet unfulfilled.

"The prince" is a Roman; he is the "little horn" of Daniel 7; he is "the beast" of Revelation 13. After the church is removed from the earth, he will make a covenant with Israel. Israel will accept him as her Messiah, but in the midst of the "week" he will break his covenant by placing an image in the temple (Rev. 13). This is the abomination of desolation. What Israel thought to be the Millennium will turn out to be the Great Tribulation (Matt. 24:15–26). Only the coming of Christ can end this frightful period (Matt. 24:27–31).

My friend, you and I are living in the age of grace, and the Seventieth Week of Daniel, the Great Tribulation, as the Lord Jesus called it, is yet to take place.

CHAPTER 10

THEME: Time, place, and preparation of Daniel for the vision; the vision of Christ glorified; transforming effect on Daniel; message of an unidentified heavenly messenger; Daniel assured and strengthened

These last three chapters should be treated as one vision. The version relates to the nation Israel in the immediate future and also in the latter days. For example, there is the historical "little horn" and also the "little horn" of the latter days.

Some expositors consider this last vision to be the greatest of all the visions of Daniel. Although it may not have such stature, it is indeed the most unique section. There are features here which are different from all other chapters. In this last vision even the method of revelation was changed.

Another outstanding feature is that it fills in much detail of the preceding visions. While all was prophetic when it was given, at the present time much has been fulfilled and belongs to history. There is also a great deal that is yet prophetic—to be fulfilled in the last days. The line of demarcation between what has been fulfilled and what is yet to be fulfilled is not always clear. We have already seen the priciple of double reference, which refers to predictions that have a near and local fulfillment and also have a distant fulfillment. Of course, the fulfillment in the *immediate* future gives us the key for the far future fulfillment. For example, the historical fulfillment in Antiochus Epiphanes gives us a picture of the future fulfillment which will be in Antichrist.

The key to understanding these last three chapters is found in the explanation the angel gives to Daniel: "Now I am come to make thee understand what shall befall thy people in the latter days: for yet the vision is for many days" (v. 14). In other words, it will be a long time before this will be fulfilled, and it concerns Daniel's people, the people of Israel. (Let me caution you against trying to put the church

in this section, because Daniel is making it very clear that he is talking about his people.)

We are moving into a very eerie section. Maybe you would call it
weird or strange. The veil of the spiritual world is partially and momentarily pulled aside, and we get a look into the unseen world.
There is nothing here to satisfy the morbid curiosity of an idle specta-
tor. However, there is enough to produce a beneficial and sobering
effect upon the humble believer similar to the effect that it produced
upon Daniel.

This intrusion into the spiritual realm introduces the believer to
the order of angels—both good and bad angels, fallen and unfallen.
We will see something about the kingdom of Satan, which is about us
today. There has been a great deal said and written about that recently.
Many people take a little fact and then add a whole lot of fiction to it.
We are going to stick to the facts that the Bible gives us here.

Apparently angels exercise a free will, since some of them by their
own volition followed Satan in his rebellion against God. Some of
these belong to the order of demons to which frequent reference is
made in the Gospels. The angels are in different orders, ranks, and
positions and have various powers and abilities. "For by him were all
things created, that are in heaven, and that are in earth, visible and
invisible, whether they be thrones, or dominions, or principalities, or
powers: all things were created by him, and for him" (Col. 1:16). This
makes a separation in God's creation, not only of that which is in
heaven and that which is in earth, but that which is visible and that
which is invisible. There is a great realm today that is invisible. We
are discovering that there are a great many things in this world of
energy that we know very little about.

We are told that He created *thrones*, which would be the archan-
gels like Michael and Gabriel and other special envoys. There are *dominions*, which would be the cherubim and seraphim. There are
principalities, which would be the generals, "the brass" of the angel
hosts. And *powers* would be the privates such as serve as guardian
angels (Heb. 1:4).

Some angels in the rank of principalities, that is, the generals, fell away to join with Satan. Notice what is said about "principalities": "For we wrestle not against flesh and blood, but against *principalities*, against powers, against the rulers of the darkness of this world, against spiritual wickedness in high places" (Eph. 6:12, italics mine).

Satan also has his angels organized according to rank. Just as one army is set over against another army, there are generals on both sides. Satan's "principalities," or generals, seem to have the oversight of nations. His "powers" are the privates of his army who are demons who seek to possess human beings. The "rulers of the darkness of this world" are demons who have charge of Satan's worldly business, and I think he has a lot of monkey-business going on down here. Then there is "spiritual wickedness" in the heavenlies, which are the demons who have charge of religion. You may not realize it, but Satan's department of religion is the largest department of all. He is in the business of religion. Many folk think Satan is against religion. No indeed, he is promoting religion—not Christ, but religion.

These two groups move in the arena of this universe in which we live. They are engaged in ceaseless warfare to capture the souls of men. We will see more of this as we go through this section.

TIME, PLACE, AND PREPARATION
OF DANIEL FOR THE VISION

In the third year of Cyrus king of Persia a thing was revealed unto Daniel, whose name was called Belteshazzar; and the thing was true, but the time appointed was long: and he understood the thing, and had understanding of the vision [Dan. 10:1].

The "third year of Cyrus" was 534 B.C., which was about four years after the vision of the Seventy Weeks. Daniel was an old man by this time and probably retired from public office.

"A thing [word] was revealed unto Daniel" suggests a new mode of communication.

"The thing [word] was true, but the time appointed was long" indicates that the final fulfillment was in the distant future, not the immediate future.

"He understood the thing [word], and had understanding of the vision" means that this vision was made crystal clear to Daniel.

In those days I Daniel was mourning three full weeks.

I ate no pleasant bread, neither came flesh nor wine in my mouth, neither did I anoint myself at all, till three whole weeks were fulfilled [Dan. 10:2-3].

Daniel didn't take a bath for three weeks!

The cause of Daniel's mourning is not told us, but we can speculate. Remember that it was the third year of Cyrus' reign, and in his first year he had made the decree which permitted Israel to return to her land (see Ezra 1:1-4). Two full years had passed and only a paltry few had returned to the land of Israel under Zerubbabel. This is before the group under Ezra and the group under Nehemiah had returned. This was a rigorous time for Daniel. It brought grief to the heart of this aged prophet of God, now past ninety, to see that his people did not want to return to their homeland. Probably retired now from active participation in office, evidently having served through the first year of Cyrus, he gave himself entirely to the service of God. He fasted for three weeks because he did not get an immediate answer to his prayer.

And in the four and twentieth day of the first month, as I was by the side of the great river, which is Hiddekel [Dan. 10:4].

Now he gives us the exact place and date when he received his vision and revelation. He was by the great river Hiddekel, which is the Tigris River. The time was the twenty-fourth of Nisan, April 24. Daniel is dealing with exact dates. This makes it difficult for the critics to wrestle with, because the one who wrote this was dealing with specific dates and he was not giving a *late* date for the Book of Daniel!

THE VISION OF CHRIST GLORIFIED

I think that Daniel saw the transfiguration of Christ before either Moses or Elijah saw it. You see, there have always been three representatives: Moses represented the Law, Elijah represented the prophets, but Daniel represented a very particular group of those who had been in exile, and now he is given this vision of the glorified Christ ahead of time for his encouragement.

> **Then I lifted up mine eyes, and looked, and behold a certain man clothed in linen, whose loins were girded with fine gold of Uphaz:**

> **His body also was like the beryl, and his face as the appearance of lightning, and his eyes as lamps of fire, and his arms and his feet like in colour to polished brass, and the voice of his words like the voice of a multitude [Dan. 10:5–6].**

This is a new method of revelation. No longer does Daniel see an image or visions of beasts or weeks. He sees a certain man. Who is that certain man? Some very excellent expositors hesitate to identify him, and they dodge the dilemma by saying he was a heavenly visitor. Well, that is really generalizing, and you can't be very wrong if you call him a heavenly visitor. But that is not an exegesis of the passage. I believe this Person is Christ.

When the Lord Jesus was on earth, He gave many parables, and some of them concerned the activity of "a certain man." That "certain man" was either God the Father or God the Son. In the verse before us the "certain man" is identified even further by His person and His dress. What a striking similarity there is to the vision of Christ after His ascension into glory as it was seen by John in the Revelation! "And I turned to see the voice that spake with me. And being turned, I saw seven golden candlesticks; And in the midst of the seven candlesticks one like unto the Son of man, clothed with a garment down to the foot, and girt about the paps with a golden girdle. His head and his hairs were white like wool, as white as snow; and his eyes were as a flame of fire; And his feet like unto fine brass, as if they burned in a furnace; and his voice as the sound of many waters. And he had in his right hand seven stars: and out of his mouth went a sharp two-edged sword: and his countenance was as the sun shineth in his strength" (Rev. 1:12–16). Now that is a vision of Christ, and I believe Daniel saw Christ—not in His preincarnation, but he saw Him as the postincarnate Christ, in His office as priestly Intercessor and Judge and the great Shepherd of the sheep. After all, both Israel and the church are called His sheep. It is interesting to recall that Moses and Elijah were present at the transfiguration of Jesus as recorded in the Gospel records, but Daniel was not present. Why? Well, I think it may be because he had already witnessed the transfiguration of Jesus, and this is the record of it.

TRANSFORMING EFFECT ON DANIEL

And I Daniel alone saw the vision: for the men that were with me saw not the vision; but a great quaking fell upon them, so that they fled to hide themselves [Dan. 10:7].

I do not think that any ordinary angel or even an archangel would have this effect upon these men.

Although others were with Daniel, he alone saw the vision. It is evident from many recorded incidents that only the Holy Spirit can identify Christ for men, and that is what He is doing for Daniel. The Lord Jesus said, "He shall glorify me: for he shall receive of mine, and shall shew it unto you" (John 16:14). The apostle Paul had a similar experience on the road to Damascus. "And the men which journeyed with him stood speechless, hearing a voice, but seeing no man. And Saul arose from the earth; and when his eyes were opened, he saw no man: but they led him by the hand, and brought him into Damascus" (Acts 9:7–8). Paul was blinded—he had seen the glorified Christ.

Therefore I was left alone, and saw this great vision, and there remained no strength in me: for my comeliness was turned in me into corruption, and I retained no strength [Dan. 10:8].

Daniel was left alone. That is the marvelous, wonderful experience of that man of God, and many have shared eagerly and joyfully a like experience. Abraham left Ur, and finally his kindred, and he was alone with God. Moses was sent to the backside of the desert of Midian, and at the burning bush he was alone with God. Elijah was disciplined by the Brook Cherith, and God was with him. Jeremiah walked a lonely path, but God was with him. John the Baptist was in the desert alone, but God was there. Paul had two years of solitary confinement on that same desert—that was God's opportunity to train him. The apostle John was exiled on the lonely isle of Patmos, but God was with him.

There are so many people who want to get together to have a great prayer meeting or other great gatherings. Friend, have you ever tried being alone? That is where God will meet with you. Take the Word of God and go off alone with Him. It will do you a lot of good.

I love speaking on my radio program. I have been asked, "Dr. McGee, are you speaking to an audience when you make those tapes?" The answer is, "No. I am all alone." I am in the studio with all the doors shut. I am alone, alone with God. It is wonderful. I think this is when God speaks to me. It is at this time that God has been able to use this weak bit of clay to get out the Word of God. He makes that Word go out, and He gives it its effectiveness.

In contrast, the ungodly and the unbeliever are gregarious. They want to go to the nightclubs to have a drink with somebody. They run in packs, and they like to have people around them. They don't like to be alone. You remember that Jacob tried to avoid being alone, but God pushed him into a corner so that one night God wrestled with him and finally crippled him in order to get him.

Now in this Scripture before us Daniel is alone with God, and he has this vision of the Lord Jesus Christ. He says, "there remained no strength in me"—it had a tremendous effect upon him.

> Yet heard I the voice of his words: and when I heard the
> voice of his words, then was I in a deep sleep on my face,
> and my face toward the ground [Dan. 10:9].

Daniel apparently lapsed into unconsciousness. I don't know how
long he was there. The Lord Jesus left him, and when Daniel regained
consciousness, he found that an angel had come and ministered to
him.

MESSAGE OF AN UNIDENTIFIED HEAVENLY MESSENGER

Daniel apparently is just sprawled down, prone on the earth. Then a
hand touches him.

> And, behold, an hand touched me, which set me upon
> my knees and upon the palms of my hands [Dan.
> 10:10].

This heavenly messenger was sent by the postincarnate Christ to answer Daniel's petition. Who could he have been? Well, I suggest that
he was Gabriel, since Gabriel was sent to Daniel on other occasions;
yet he could have been any other angel.

> And he said unto me, O Daniel, a man greatly beloved,
> understand the words that I speak unto thee, and stand
> upright: for unto thee am I now sent. And when he had
> spoken this word unto me, I stood trembling [Dan.
> 10:11].

You see, at first Daniel was horizontal with the ground. Then he was
brought up on all fours, and now he is told to stand up.
  "A man greatly beloved"—again Daniel is reminded of the fact
that he is greatly beloved of God. That is a nice reputation to have in
heaven, by the way!

Then said he unto me, Fear not, Daniel; for from the first day that thou didst set thine heart to understand, and to chasten thyself before thy God, thy words were heard, and I am come for thy words.

But the prince of the kingdom of Persia withstood me one and twenty days: but, lo, Michael, one of the chief princes, came to help me; and I remained there with the kings of Persia [Dan. 10:12–13].

Here a veil is lifted momentarily, and it reveals a heavenly warfare going on. It reveals there is a great deal more about this universe in which we live than meets the eye. There is a great deal more to it than we know. Very little is revealed to us, and we should not try to know more than is revealed about the unseen world.

This reveals that in the world which is unseen by us there is a conflict going on, a conflict of the ages between good and evil, light and darkness, God and Satan. It reveals that there are satanic forces and heavenly forces.

"From the first day . . . thy words were heard, and I am come for thy words." The angel is saying that Daniel's prayer was heard immediately and he was sent as a messenger with an answer. But on the way his pathway was blocked; he couldn't get through to Daniel. This is an amazing statement! This throws some light on what Paul said to the Ephesian believers: "Put on the whole armour of God, that ye may be able to stand against the wiles of the devil. For we wrestle not against flesh and blood, but against principalities, against powers, against the rulers of the darkness of this world, against spiritual wickedness in high places" (Eph. 6:11–12).

Again, here are the gradations of rank in the forces of Satan. Their power may explain the reason your prayer and my prayer have not yet been answered. Actually, prayer is fighting a spiritual battle always. Paul made it clear that prayer was a spiritual battle for him. "Now I beseech you, brethren, for the Lord Jesus Christ's sake, and for the love of the Spirit, that ye strive together with me in your prayers to

God for me" (Rom. 15:30). "Strive together" is the Greek word
sunagōnizom—from this root we get our English word agonize. You
and I are to agonize in prayer.

Prayer has been made a light sort of thing today. Most of the prayers I hear are either very flowery or very theological, and I think we
could do without both kinds. Real prayer is agonizing. It is getting
through the barriers to release spiritual power. It is not done by trying
to entertain the Lord with flowery language or by trying to be very
profound and theological. My friend, we are fighting a spiritual battle!

Again, the angel said to Daniel, "When you began to pray, God
sent me to answer your prayer, but I couldn't get through to you because on the way the prince of the kingdom of Persia withstood me for
twenty-one days." Who is he? No earthly or human prince could do
such a thing. This evidently was an envoy of Satan, one of the demons. We know that God has His angels organized, and apparently
Satan also has his demons organized like an army. There are the generals and the colonels, the lieutenants and second lieutenants, ser-
geants and corporals, and so on. Apparently this angel was outranked
by the satanic angel who was the prince of the kingdom of Persia, and
so he couldn't get through and had to send back for reinforcements. In
fact, Michael, the archangel, had to come to open up the way for him.

Why would the way be blocked? Daniel is going to be given information about the kingdom of Persia and about the kingdom of
Greece—we will see that when we get to the next chapter. Satan didn't
want that kind of information to get out. It was secret information that
he didn't want released to the human family. But God wanted the information to be gotten through to Daniel.

"Michael, one of the chief princes, came to help me; and I remained there with the kings of Persia." Apparently there was a conflict going on involving the kings of Persia (remember that Daniel was
in Persia), and there needed to be some heavenly forces to help. This
was about the time that Daniel had the experience of being put into
the den of lions. You see, the Lord was active on Daniel's behalf without his knowing anything about it.

Oh, my friend, we need to recognize as believers that we are in a spiritual warfare. It is amazing how many times the Devil short-circuits our prayer life.

One of the reasons that public prayer and prayer meetings are so dead is because those who go there say some pretty little prayers without realizing that there is a battle going on. There is a *war* that must be fought and won. Paul mentions this again in 2 Corinthians 10:3–5: "For though we walk in the flesh, we do not war after the flesh: (For the weapons of our warfare are not carnal, but mighty through God to the pulling down of strong holds;) Casting down imaginations, and every high thing that exalteth itself against the knowledge of God, and bringing into captivity every thought to the obedience of Christ."

Friend, the Christian life is a bigger undertaking than any of us ever dreamed it to be. You and I need to recognize how much we need the power of the Holy Spirit in our lives and how much we need the presence of Christ. We need to be more conscious of the fact that we are engaged in a spiritual warfare. *important*

> **Now I am come to make thee understand what shall befall thy people in the latter days: for yet the vision is for many days [Dan. 10:14].**

This is the key which opens the door to the understanding of the remainder of the Book of Daniel. There are three features which characterize this closing vision.

1. The vision concerns "thy people." I think we can dogmatically and categorically identify the prophecy as having Israel as its subject. If anyone tries to interpret this in any other way, then semantics and syntax are meaningless. "Thy people" means Israel.

2. It will be accomplished "in the latter days." This places the final fulfillment in the period of the Seventieth Week, which is the time of the Great Tribulation period. The "latter days" places it at the end of that period.

3. "Yet the vision is for many days." This emphasizes the fact that a long period of time is involved—not only in fulfillment—but before the vision will be finalized.

We will come to the two parts of the vision: the historical (it was prophetic when it was given, but now has been fulfilled) and the prophecy yet to be fulfilled.

DANIEL ASSURED AND STRENGTHENED

And when he had spoken such words unto me, I set my face toward the ground, and I became dumb.

And, behold, one like the similitude of the sons of men touched my lips: then I opened my mouth, and spake, and said unto him that stood before me, O my lord, by the vision my sorrows are turned upon me, and I have retained no strength [Dan. 10:15–16].

This was having a tremendous effect upon Daniel physically, as you can see.

For how can the servant of this my lord talk with this my lord? for as for me, straightway there remained no strength in me, neither is there breath left in me.

Then there came again and touched me one like the appearance of a man, and he strengthened me [Dan. 10:17–18].

When I hear people today tell me that they have had a vision of an angel but it doesn't seem to have affected them very much, I know they didn't really see an angel. The experience of seeing an angel certainly had a tremendous effect upon Daniel.

And said, O man greatly beloved, fear not: peace be unto thee, be strong, yea, be strong. And when he had spoken unto me, I was strengthened, and said, Let my lord speak; for thou hast strengthened me.

Then said he, Knowest thou wherefore I come unto thee? and now will I return to fight with the prince of Persia:

> and when I am gone forth, lo, the prince of Grecia shall
> come [Dan. 10:19–20].

Another angel that represents Greece will come—another satanic
principality. The angel who was speaking to Daniel had to get back to
the battle that was going on.

> But I will shew thee that which is noted in the scripture
> of truth: and there is none that holdeth with me in these
> things, but Michael your prince [Dan. 10:21].

"That which is noted in the scripture of truth"—the angel turns Daniel to the Word of God. Noted means "recorded or registered." In other
words, Daniel will not hear or see anything that is contradictory to the
Word of God.

My friend, the Word of God is the only weapon available to the
child of God for effective use in our spiritual warfare. It is called the
sword of the Spirit, and some of us don't know how to use our swords.

CHAPTER 11

THEME: Vision continued; Antiochus Epiphanes identified; vicious and vocal volition of the Man of Sin; victory of the willful king is temporary

Chapters 10—12 all deal with the same vision, and therefore chapter 11 is a continuation of the previous chapter. It is a very important chapter because it fills in some of the details of the Seventy Weeks of chapter 9, which specifically concern Daniel's people, Israel. It also fills in some of the details of the last three of the four nations symbolized in the multimetallic image of chapter 2 and in the beasts of chapter 7. The very importance of this chapter caused Satan to hinder the angel in coming to give Daniel the answer to his prayer, because this prophecy does concern two of the nations which were all-important in relation to Daniel's people. The two nations were Persia and Greece.

A further notable contribution of this chapter is that it bridges prophetically part of the gap between the Old and New Testaments. We speak of the intertestamental period between the Old and New Testaments as being a period of silence, which is not exactly accurate. The intertestamental period was the time of Israel's greatest travail. They suffered at the hands of both Syria and Egypt. As these two nations warred against each other, Palestine was caught in the middle as the armies of these two nations seesawed back and forth, up and down, across the land of Israel.

During the intertestamental period came the rise of Antiochus Epiphanes (who is a type of the Antichrist of the future). He was a member of the Seleucid family, and we will identify him when we come to him in this chapter. He was a persecutor of the Jews, far exceeding any Pharaoh or Haman or Hitler or modern Russia. He has been called the Nero of Jewish history. He has also been called the Great Profaner.

There is a remarkable division in the chapter which separates history and prophecy—the historical from the eschatological section. Remember, it was all future when it was originally written, but part of it has been fulfilled.

This prophecy is rather complicated and goes into prophecy a little deeper than the average person likes to go into it. Most people seem to like the exciting, sensational part of prophecy, but they do not want to dig down into the Word of God to see what it really says. However, if you are one who enjoys a deep and detailed study of prophecy, you will be thrilled by this section of the remarkable Word of God.

important ✓

VISION CONTINUED

This prophecy bridges the gap from Media-Persia over to Greece, from Asia to Europe. It tells of the transition of world powers from one continent to another, from the East to the West. Remember that the prophecy concerns the people of Daniel. It was especially important to Israel because they would be caught in a vise between these different powers. It would be a period of great suffering for these people.

Also I in the first year of Darius the Mede, even I, stood to confirm and to strengthen him [Dan. 11:1].

The speaker here is the angel, and this is a continuation from chapter 10. The angel may have been Gabriel; we are not told his name. Remember that it occurred during the reign of Darius when Daniel was thrown into the den of lions. Darius tried in vain to deliver Daniel, but he was trapped by his own decree. Yet he said to Daniel, "Thy God whom thou servest continually, he will deliver thee" (Dan. 6:16).

"I stood to confirm and strengthen him." The angel confirmed and strengthened Darius in his faith. He also comforted and assisted Daniel. And Daniel said, you recall, "My God hath sent his angel, and hath shut the lions' mouths" (Dan. 6:22).

So historically this is where the vision fits in, and it bridges the gap between the Old and New Testaments, the intertestamental period.

> And now will I shew thee the truth. Behold, there shall
> stand up yet three kings in Persia; and the fourth shall
> be far richer than they all: and by his strength through
> his riches he shall stir up all against the realm of Grecia
> [Dan. 11:2].

From here through verse 34 is one of the most remarkable examples of
prewritten history. This section has caused the destructive critic to
demand a late date for the composition of the Book of Daniel. Here are
clear-cut statements of prophecy which have been literally fulfilled.

The prophecy of this chapter is so detailed and so accurate that the
liberal critic will not accept the fact that it was written before it happened. He insists that Daniel's prophecy was written after it had become history. Personally, I do not like the liberals to be called liberal.
To me they are the most narrow-minded people I know anything
about. Yet they like to speak of their broad-mindedness and that they
don't have a narrow conception of Scripture. Let me give you an example. One of them right here in Southern California said to me,
"McGee, I listen to you on the radio sometimes." (He said that in a
condescending manner as though I should have been honored.) Then
he said, "I notice that you accept prophecy as being reliable," and he
cited this Book of Daniel. So I asked him, "What authority do you
have for rejecting the early dating of Daniel and accepting a late date
of Daniel?" His reply was this, "Well, it's very simple. We know that
miracles are impossible, that they do not happen. Therefore if this
were written beforehand, it would be a miracle; so it must have been
written afterward." Now, my friend, I ask you, is that being narrow-
minded, prejudiced, and biased? Obviously, this chapter before us is
one of the most remarkable passages of prewritten history in the Word
of God, and conservative scholarship can sustain the early date of
Daniel. This means that you have a miracle on your hands.

When the angel gave this information to Daniel, he knew that Daniel would not live to see it fulfilled. Obviously, it was recorded for the
comfort and encouragement of the people of God who would live
through the difficult days it describes. Also it was written for all gen-

erations as a testimony to the fact that God knows the end from the beginning.

The angel told him that there would be four notable kings of Persia to follow Cyrus. We think we can identify them today: (1) Cambyses, 529 B.C. (2) Pseudo-Smerdis, 522 B.C. (3) Darius Hystaspis, 521 B.C. (4) Xerxes who invaded Greece in 480 B.C. He was defeated, and never again did Medo-Persia make a bid for world dominion. Incidentally, I believe that Xerxes is the Ahasuerus of the Book of Esther. He was very rich, as the prophecy here said he would be.

> **And a mighty king shall stand up, that shall rule with great dominion, and do according to his will [Dan. 11:3].**

"A mighty king" is Alexander the Great who came to power in 335 B.C. over the Graeco-Macedonian Empire. He put down Persia and assumed world dominion.

> **And when he shall stand up, his kingdom shall be broken, and shall be divided toward the four winds of heaven; and not to his posterity, nor according to his dominion which he ruled: for his kingdom shall be plucked up, even for others beside those [Dan. 11:4].**

Alexander the Great was a world ruler and probably the greatest military strategist the world has ever seen, but he died an alcoholic in 323 B.C. His own posterity did not inherit his vast kingdom. Four of his generals divided the empire into four geographical areas, each ruled by one general. The division was roughly this: Cassander took Macedonia; Lysimachus took Asia Minor (modern Turkey); Seleucus Nicator took Syria and the remainder of the Middle East; and Ptolemy took Egypt. All four families warred among themselves. Eventually they all lost their kingdoms when the Romans marched east.

> And the king of the south shall be strong, and one of his
> princes; and he shall be strong above him, and have do-
> minion; his dominion shall be a great dominion [Dan.
> 11:5].

King of Egypt

"The king of the south." South of what? Directions in the Bible are
reckoned from Palestine as the center of the earth. The king of the
south is not from south of Los Angeles or Chicago or New York. It is
the king from the south of Israel, so this would be the king from
Egypt. This king of the south would be one of the Ptolemies.

> And in the end of years they shall join themselves to-
> gether; for the king's daughter of the south shall come to
> the king of the north to make an agreement: but she
> shall not retain the power of the arm; neither shall he
> stand, nor his arm: but she shall be given up, and they
> that brought her, and he that begat her, and he that
> strengthened her in these times [Dan. 11:6].

"The king of the north" refers to the line of the Seleucidae. This verse
brings us to about 250 B.C. Although historians differ on some of the
minor details, they have recorded some of the manipulations that
went on in the courts of that day, which fulfill this prophecy very
accurately. To form an alliance between these two warring families,
Ptolemy Philadelphus of Egypt gave his daughter Berenice in marriage to Antiochus Theos of Syria. Antiochus was already married to
Laodice, whom he divorced. After two years Ptolemy Philadelphus
died; so Antiochus Theos put away Berenice with her son and took
back his first wife, Laodice. She, in turn, poisoned Antiochus Theos
and ordered the death of Berenice and her son. The Laodice put her
own son, Seleucus Callinicus, on the throne. That was some juggling
act, and it is interesting how this is covered in the prophecy given to
Daniel.

> But out of a branch of her roots shall one stand up in his
> estate, which shall come with an army, and shall enter

into the fortress of the king of the north, and shall deal
against them, and shall prevail [Dan. 11:7].

Eu frah-Tees

This was Ptolemy Euergetes, brother of Berenice, who came with an
army and captured Syria, and he seized the fort which was the port of
Antioch in that day.

And shall also carry captives into Egypt their gods,
with their princes, and with their precious vessels of
silver and of gold; and he shall continue more years
than the king of the north.

So the king of the south shall come into his kingdom,
and shall return into his own land [Dan. 11:8–9].

Tol'eh-me Eu-frah-Tees

It is recorded that Ptolemy Euergetes took into Egypt as booty four
thousand talents of gold, forty thousand talents of silver, and twenty-
five hundred idols. Do you see how this scripture was literally fulfilled?

But his sons shall be stirred up, and shall assemble a
multitude of great forces: and one shall certainly come,
and overflow, and pass through: then shall he return,
and be stirred up, even to his fortress.

And the king of the south shall be moved with choler,
and shall come forth and fight with him, even with the
king of the north: and he shall set forth a great multitude; but the multitude shall be given into his hands.

And when he hath taken away the multitude, his heart
shall be lifted up; and he shall cast down many ten
thousands: but he shall not be strengthened by it.

For the king of the north shall return, and shall set forth
a multitude greater than the former, and shall certainly
come after certain years with a great army and with
much riches [Dan. 11:10–13].

There was continual warfare between Egypt and Syria. Without going into detail, let me say that during this period Israel seemed repeatedly to make the wrong choice and found herself being made captive first by one, then by the other.

> **And in those times there shall many stand up against the king of the south: also the robbers of thy people shall exalt themselves to establish the vision; but they shall fall [Dan. 11:14].**

Many in the nation of Israel were slain at this time. They incurred untold suffering from both the king of the north and the king of the south.

> **So the king of the north shall come, and cast up a mount, and take the most fenced cities: and the arms of the south shall not withstand, neither his chosen people, neither shall there be any strength to withstand.**

> **But he that cometh against him shall do according to his own will, and none shall stand before him: and he shall stand in the glorious land, which by his hand shall be consumed [Dan. 11:15–16].**

"He shall stand in the glorious land." Now we know why this has been recorded and given to Daniel—it concerns the "glorious land," which is Israel, the land that God had vouchsafed to Abraham and to those coming after him.

These two verses predict what history now records as the victory of Antiochus the Great over Egypt. It was a decisive victory, and it caused Israel to suffer immeasurably. I am going to pass over some of the secular history of this period. If you care to go into detail, I suggest that you consult one of the larger Bible encyclopedias, such as *Hastings'* or the *International Standard Bible Encyclopedia*, and read in detail the secular history covered in this section. You will find that

Daniel's prophecy was fulfilled in a remarkable way. There is a period of 125 years that was fulfilled in detail.

> **He shall also set his face to enter with the strength of his whole kingdom, and upright ones with him; thus shall he do: and he shall give him the daughter of women, corrupting her: but she shall not stand on his side, neither be for him [Dan. 11:17].**

This brings us to about 198 or 195 B.C. when Antiochus the Great made a treaty with Egypt and gave his daughter Cleopatra to Ptolemy Epiphanes in marriage. *To-leh-me*

> **After this shall he turn his face unto the isles, and shall take many: but a prince for his own behalf shall cause the reproach offered by him to cease; without his own reproach he shall cause it to turn upon him.**

> **Then he shall turn his face toward the fort of his own land: but he shall stumble and fall, and not be found.**

> **Then shall stand up in his estate a raiser of taxes in the glory of the kingdom: but within few days he shall be destroyed, neither in anger, nor in battle [Dan. 11:18–20].**

"He shall turn his face unto the isles" refers to Greece and all the Greek islands. This is where Antiochus the Great was beginning to move at this time—not only against Ptolemy in the south, but against Lysimachus in the west. *To-leh-me*

"A prince for his own behalf" would refer to another line, that is, Rome, which was beginning to arise in the west and move toward the east. Rome, you see, exacted taxes from the Syrians. The Romans were probably the best tax assessors and tax gatherers in the world until modern America perfected the system. Our system of collecting taxes would put even Rome to shame! As Rome began to rise, she was building a tremendous empire by taxing the people she was capturing. As the Syrians began to fall before Rome, there were many historical details that could be filled in. For further reading I would suggest to you *The Prophet Daniel* by A. C. Gaebelein and *The Coming Prince* by Sir Robert Anderson, a former chief of Scotland Yard.

ANTIOCHUS EPIPHANES IDENTIFIED

Introduced to us now is the vile person, Antiochus Epiphanes, who was king in Syria and is easily identified in history.

This is the "little horn" that has already been fulfilled, as we studied back in chapter 8.

> **And in his estate shall stand up a vile person, to whom they shall not give the honour of the kingdom: but he shall come in peaceably, and obtain the kingdom by flatteries [Dan. 11:21].**

This prophecy is concerned with one king in the line of the Seleucidae, Antiochus Epiphanes. Most fundamental interpreters of Scripture consider this section to be a direct reference to this man. The prophecy fits the history of Antiochus Epiphanes like a glove. (He is at the same time a type of the Antichrist, thus illustrative and figurative of the Man of Sin who is yet to come. The careers of both are strikingly similar.)

Antiochus Epiphanes came to the throne in 175 B.C. He is called vile because of his blasphemies. He came to the throne with a program of peace. (The Antichrist will come to power in the same way. He will introduce the Great Tribulation with three and one half years of peace, and the people of the world will think they are entering the Millennium when they are really entering the Great Tribulation period.) Antiochus was a deceiver and a flatterer. My friend, beware of that type of person. You can find them even in the ministry. They have hurt the church more than anything. We do not need men who will deceive and butter up folk for their own advantage; we need honest, forthright men who will stand in the pulpit and tell it like it is. Unfor-

tunately, they are getting few and far between, but, thank God, there
are still many of them about.

> And with the arms of a flood shall they be overflown
> from before him, and shall be broken; yea, also the
> prince of the covenant.
>
> And after the league made with him he shall work de-
> ceitfully: for he shall come up, and shall become strong
> with a small people.
>
> He shall enter peaceably even upon the fattest places of
> the province; and he shall do that which his fathers have
> not done, nor his fathers' fathers; he shall scatter among
> them the prey, and spoil, and riches: yea, and he shall
> forecast his devices against the strong holds, even for a
> time [Dan. 11:22–24].

"The prince of the covenant" was probably the high priest, Onias III,
who was deposed and murdered at this time by the deceitful devices
of Antiochus when he came to power.

> And he shall stir up his power and his courage against
> the king of the south with a great army; and the king of
> the south shall be stirred up to battle with a very great
> and mighty army; but he shall not stand: for they shall
> forecast devices against him.
>
> Yea, they that feed of the portion of his meat shall de-
> stroy him, and his army shall overflow: and many shall
> fall down slain.
>
> And both these kings' hearts shall be to do mischief, and
> they shall speak lies at one table; but it shall not pros-
> per: for yet the end shall be at the time appointed.
>
> Then shall he return into his land with great riches; and
> his heart shall be against the holy covenant; and he

shall do exploits, and return to his own land [Dan. 11:25–28].

These verses describe the campaign of Antiochus and his victory over the king of Egypt, which brought him much riches and prestige.

"They shall speak lies at one table" refers to the fact that he was an unreliable liar. It also reveals that the conference tables of that day were very much like the conference tables of our own day, where nations meet and make treaties which become meaningless scraps of paper.

> **At the time appointed he shall return, and come toward the south; but it shall not be as the former, or as the latter.**
>
> **For the ships of Chittim shall come against him: therefore he shall be grieved, and returned, and have indignation against the holy covenant: so shall he do; he shall even return, and have intelligence with them that forsake the holy covenant [Dan. 11:29–30].**

Antiochus made a second campaign against Egypt but was not successful due to the navy of Rome, "the ships of Chittim." He broke his covenant with Israel, but notice that some of the Jews betrayed their own people—"he shall even return, and have intelligence with them that forsake the holy covenant."

> **And arms shall stand on his part, and they shall pollute the sanctuary of strength, and shall take away the daily sacrifice, and they shall place the abomination that maketh desolate [Dan. 11:31].**

Antiochus came against Jerusalem in 170 B.C., at which time over one hundred thousand Jews were slain! He took away the daily sacrifice from the temple, offered the blood and broth of a swine upon the altar, and set up an image of Jupiter to be worshiped in the holy place of the temple of God. This was an "abomination that maketh desolate," but it was not the abomination to which our Lord Jesus referred which was future when He was on earth and is still future in our day. It is the abomination which Antichrist will set up. Antiochus set up an image of Jupiter in the holy place, and the Antichrist will probably set up an image of himself in the holy place.

> **And such as do wickedly against the covenant shall he corrupt by flatteries: but the people that do know their God shall be strong, and do exploits [Dan. 11:32].**

There were a few in the nation Israel who played the role of Judas, but there were many who knew God and were strong and did exploits. It was during this time that God raised up the family of the Maccabees. In 166 B.C. Mattathias the priest raised a revolt against the awful blasphemy. The family was called the Maccabees, that is, the hammer. Although they are not recorded in Scripture, I am convinced that they were God's men for that particular hour.

> **And they that understand among the people shall instruct many: yet they shall fall by the sword, and by flame, by captivity, and by spoil, many days.**
>
> **Now when they shall fall, they shall be holpen with a little help: but many shall cleave to them with flatteries [Dan. 11:33–34].**

This period lies between the Testaments and is a saga of suffering. There were many in this time who served God as faithfully and courageously as had Gideon or David or Elijah or Jeremiah or Daniel. If you are not familiar with this period of history, you should look into the apocryphal books of 1 and 2 Maccabees as well as the writings of Josephus.

> **And some of them of understanding shall fall, to try them, and to purge, and to make them white, even to the**

time of the end: because it is yet for a time appointed
[Dan. 11:35].

"The time of the end" leaps forward in prophecy from Antiochus
Epiphanes to the Antichrist. We move now from the history of that day
into that which is yet in the future. All of this prophecy was in the
future when Daniel gave it—some is now history and some is yet future.

VICIOUS AND VOCAL VOLITION
OF THE MAN OF SIN

**And the king shall do according to his will; and he shall
exalt himself, and magnify himself above every god,
and shall speak marvellous things against the God of
gods, and shall prosper till the indignation be accomplished: for that that is determined shall be done [Dan.
11:36].**

ends lesson 11

At this point history ends and prophecy begins. The text passes from
a vile person to a vicious character, moving over a bridge of unmea-
sured time. Antiochus Epiphanes was certainly a contemptible person, but he could not measure up to the king described in verses
36–39. Antiochus was an adumbration of Antichrist, and I believe
that this passage of Scripture thus indicates that Antichrist will rise
out of the geographical bounds of the ancient Grecian Empire.

There will be a political Antichrist, the one who is mentioned
here, a Gentile raised out of the Roman Empire. There will also be a
religious Antichrist who will pretend to be Christ and who will arise
out of the land of Israel—he will be like a wolf in sheep's clothing.

Antichrist is given many names in Scripture. J. Dwight Pentecost,
in his book *Things to Come* (p. 334), gives a list of names compiled by
Arthur W. Pink (*The Antichrist*, pp. 59–75) which are applicable to
Antichrist: "The Bloody and Deceitful Man (Ps. 5:6), the Wicked One
(Ps. 10:2–4), the Man of the Earth (Ps. 10:18), the Mighty Man (Ps.
52:1), the Enemy (Ps. 55:3), the Adversary (Ps. 74:8–10), the Head of

Many Countries (Ps. 111:6 [sic]), the Violent Man (Psalm 140:1), the Assyrian (Isa. 10:5-12), the King of Babylon (Isa. 14:2), the Sun [sic] of the Morning (Isa. 14:12), the Spoiler (Isa. 16:4-5; Jer. 6:26), the Nail (Isa. 22:25), the Branch of the Terrible Ones (Isa. 25:5), the Profane Wicked Prince of Israel (Ezek. 21:25-27), the Little Horn (Dan. 7:8), the Prince that shall come (Dan. 9:26), the Vile Person (Dan. 11:21), the Willful King (Dan. 11:36), the Idol Shepherd (Zech. 11:16-17), the Man of Sin (2 Thess. 2:3), the Son of Perdition (2 Thess. 2:3), the Lawless one (2 Thess. 2:8), the Antichrist (1 John 2:22), the Angels [sic] of the Bottomless Pit (Rev. 9:11), the Beast (Rev. 11:7; 13:1). To these could be added: the One Coming in His Own Name (John 5:43), the King of Fierce Countenance (Dan. 8:23), the Abomination of Desolation (Matt. 24:15), the Desolator (Dan. 9:27)."

"The king shall do according to his will." Antichrist is self-willed. How contrary this is to the Lord Jesus Christ who said, "I can of mine own self do nothing: as I hear, I judge: and my judgment is just; because I seek not mine own will, but the will of the Father which hath sent me" (John 5:30).

"He shall exalt himself." The little horn (the name given to Antichrist in ch. 7) tries to be a big horn. Again, how unlike the Lord Jesus this is! Paul wrote of Him: "Let this mind be in you, which was also in Christ Jesus: Who, being in the form of God, thought it not robbery to be equal with God: But made himself of no reputation, and took upon him the form of a servant, and was made in the likeness of men: And being found in fashion as a man, he humbled himself, and became obedient unto death, even the death of the cross" (Phil 2:5-8).

"And magnify himself above every god." In 2 Thessalonians 2:4 Paul wrote of the Antichrist: "Who opposeth and exalteth himself above all that is called God, or that is worshipped; so that he as God sitteth in the temple of God, shewing himself that he is God." And in Revelation 13:8 we are also told: "And all that dwell upon the earth shall worship him, whose names are not written in the book of life of the Lamb slain from the foundation of the world."

It is blasphemous rebellion against God which marks the willful king as the final and logical expression of humanism. He is the typical representative of that which is against God and that which is our old nature: "Because the carnal mind is enmity against God: for it is not subject to the law of God, neither indeed can be. So then they that are in the flesh cannot please God" (Rom. 8:7–8). The carnal mind of men will turn to the Antichrist. When men choose their own rulers and leaders, what kind of man do they choose? Generally it is one who is like they are, and that is the reason we are getting such sorry leaders in the world today. The leadership of the world is frightful—they are the kind of folk we picked out. God has said right here in the Book of Daniel that He would set over the kingdoms of this world the basest of rulers.

"And shall prosper till the indignation be accomplished." The willful king will be successful at first and for a brief time. God will permit this to come to pass during the last half of Daniel's Seventieth Week.

> **Neither shall he regard the God of his fathers, nor the desire of women, nor regard any god: for he shall magnify himself above all [Dan. 11:37].**

"Neither shall he regard the God of his fathers." It has been assumed from this statement that Antichrist would have to be an Israelite. However, this statement could refer to a Protestant, a Roman Catholic, or a heathen. Wherever he comes from, he will not regard the God of his fathers. We have examples of this in history. Smith, the head of the now defunct organization the American Association for the Advancement of Atheism, was the son of a Methodist minister, and Stalin at one time studied in a theological seminary.

As I have stated previously, I believe that it takes two men to fulfill this office, and they are both presented in chapter 13 of Revelation. This first one is a political ruler who comes out of the Roman Empire and probably the Greek section of the Roman Empire. He is the one who doesn't have to be an Israelite at all. The second beast that arises is a religious leader, and he imitates Christ—I assume he will be an Israelite.

"Nor the desire of women." This refers evidently to the desire of Hebrew women to be the mother of the Messiah. Not only will the

Lord Jesus Christ be absolutely rejected, He will become the enemy. Antichrist leads a rebellion against God and Christ. As Psalm 2 puts it: "The kings of the earth set themselves, and the rulers take counsel together, against the LORD, and against his anointed, saying, Let us break their bands asunder, and cast away their cords from us" (Ps. 2:2–3).

"Nor regard any god." That means very plainly that he will oppose all religions and worship, except worship of himself. He is not only a believer in the ecumenical movement, he promotes it; in fact, he is it. One religion for one world will be his motto, and he is that religion.

"He shall magnify himself above all" is the final fruition of the self-will of this willful king. His total ambition is self-adulation.

This is the frightful prospect of the final days of the Great Tribulation period: "And he had power to give life unto the image of the beast, that image of the beast should both speak, and cause that as many as would not worship the image of the beast should be killed. And he causeth all, both small and great, rich and poor, free and bond, to receive a mark in their right hand, or in their foreheads: And that no man might buy or sell, save he that had the mark, or the name of the beast, or the number of his name" (Rev. 13:15–17). You will not be able to go to a restaurant to eat or buy a ticket on a plane or train without the mark of the Beast. I tell you, that is going to be dictatorship with a vengeance!

> **But in his estate shall he honour the God of forces: and a god whom his fathers knew not shall he honour with gold, and silver, and with precious stones, and pleasant things [Dan. 11:38].**

"The God of forces" should be more accurately translated "the God of fortresses." It is true that we are living in a day, as someone has written, in which man is increasingly making gods out of forces, but that is not what Daniel is saying here. I am quoting Dr. Newell: "We know from pagan mythology that both Cybele and Diana are variously represented as crowned with multi-tiered crowns, plainly setting forth the idea of fortification with turrets, battlements, and so forth" (*Dan-*

ie1, *The Man Greatly Beloved, and His Prophecies,* p. 179). I am sure
you have seen pictures of these heathen idols with their multi-tiered
crowns with all kinds of fortresses on them which represent the kingdoms of this world. Antichrist will honor the god of fortresses who
had the kingdoms of the world. Who is that? Well, it was Satan who
offered to Christ the kingdoms of this world, and our Lord rejected his
offer. Apparently, Satan had a right to make that offer. Antichrist will
accept the offer and become the world's dictator. We are told in
2 Thessalonians 2:4 and Revelation 13:4 that Antichrist will accept
worship and will have the world worshiping Satan in that day. All the
kingdoms of the world will be under his rulership, the first truly
worldwide dictatorship.

> **Thus shall he do in the most strong holds with a strange
> god, whom he shall acknowledge and increase with
> glory: and he shall cause them to rule over many, and
> shall divide the land for gain [Dan. 11:39].**

This is going to be Satan's hour. He will make the most of it, as he
knows his time is short. "Therefore rejoice, ye heavens, and ye that
dwell in them. Woe to the inhabiters of the earth and of the sea! for the
devil is come down unto you, having great wrath, because he knoweth that he hath but a short time" (Rev. 12:12). Antichrist will be the
pliant tool to completely do the will of Satan in that day. He will rule
over many people and dispose of property as he pleases. He is the
willful king and the final world dictator.

VICTORY OF THE WILLFUL KING IS TEMPORARY

> **And at the time of the end shall the king of the south
> push at him: and the king of the north shall come
> against him like a whirlwind, with chariots, and with
> horsemen, and with many ships; and he shall enter into
> the countries, and shall overflow and pass over [Dan.
> 11:40].**

It is "the time of the end," not the end of time. It is the end which Daniel has had in mind all through this section, the last days of the nation Israel, which the Lord Jesus labeled the Great Tribulation.

"The king of the south" is evidently a ruler of Egypt, but it is impossible for us to identify him. Actually, Egypt has not had a native ruler for years. God has done a pretty good job of putting over that nation the basest of rulers. However, this one who is going to arise at the time of the end will probably unite all of Africa as no leader of Egypt has ever been able to do, and he will come against Antichrist.

"The king of the north" is more easily identified. He takes the place of the Seleucidae dynasty, and I believe he is the one who comes out of the north mentioned in Ezekiel 38 and 39. The king of the north is Russia. Russia will open the campaign of Armageddon which will not be just a battle, but an entire war. At the very beginning, the king of the north will be eliminated as God moves in judgment upon that nation.

> **He shall enter also into the glorious land, and many countries shall be overthrown: but these shall escape out of his hand, even Edom, and Moab, and the chief of the children of Ammon [Dan. 11:41].**

The entrance of Russia into Palestine precipitates the great crisis and conflict of the Great Tribulation period.

When Antichrist enters Palestine, that is, "the glorious land," he will find that he is going to have trouble with Edom, Moab, and Ammon. That is the territory where the sons of Ishmael, the Arabs, are today. He is going to have trouble with them, for a while at least.

> **He shall stretch forth his hand also upon the countries: and the land of Egypt shall not escape [Dan. 11:42].**

Egypt and the king of the south will yield to the Antichrist.

> But he shall have power over the treasures of gold and of silver, and over all the precious things of Egypt: and the Libyans and the Ethiopians shall be at his steps [Dan. 11:43].

He will have control of the wealth of this world. He will control the entire money markets of the world at that time. Libya and Ethiopia will surrender to him—he will have control of Africa.

> But tidings out of the east and out of the north shall trouble him: therefore he shall go forth with great fury to destroy, and utterly to make away many [Dan. 11:44].

"Tidings out of the east"—that means the Orient with its teeming millions. A great army will come from there to the Battle of Armageddon, and this world ruler will be troubled. At that time, there will be no hope for God's people, except in God Himself.

> And he shall plant the tabernacles of his palace between the seas in the glorious holy mountain; yet he shall come to his end, and none shall help him [Dan. 11:45].

"The seas" refer to the Mediterranean Sea, and "the glorious holy mountain" is Jerusalem. In other words, at that time Antichrist will establish his headquarters for world conquest between the Mediterranean Sea and Jerusalem. However, instead of ruling from there he will be destroyed by the personal return of the Lord Jesus Christ (Rev. 19:17–20). Evil will have taken over, and only in the personal coming of Christ to establish His Kingdom will any on this earth be delivered and saved.

CHAPTER 12

THEME: *The Great Tribulation; the resurrections of Old Testament saints and sinners; sealing of prophecy till the time of the end; the abomination of desolation*

Chapter 12 now concludes the vision which began back in chapter 10. This is all one vision, and everything about it must fit together like a jigsaw puzzle. The problem is that some people dip into this prophecy here and there, making applications as they see fit. We need to remember that this is all one vision, and we were told concerning it: "Now I am come to make thee understand what shall befall thy people in the latter days: for yet the vision is for many days" (Dan. 10:14). There are three important things that we note from this verse:

1. "Thy people" means that it concerns the nation Israel after the church is removed from the earth.

2. It is "in the latter days." The latter days of the Old Testament are identified with the last days of the New Testament which the Lord Jesus called the Great Tribulation period and which correspond to the Seventieth Week of Daniel.

3. "Yet the vision is for many days," that is, there will be a long time before you come to the latter days. It has been a long time since Daniel had these visions; in fact, at least twenty-five hundred years have gone by. Whether we are moving in the orbit of these days, I do not know. The church will have to be removed first—that is the next happening in the program of God. We have no date for that—we have no sign for it. Anyone who tries to set a date for the Rapture is dealing with something that is not found in the Word of God.

THE GREAT TRIBULATION

And at that time shall Michael stand up, the great prince which standeth for the children of thy people:

**and there shall be a time of trouble, such as never was
since there was a nation even to that same time: and at
that time thy people shall be delivered, every one that
shall be found written in the book [Dan. 12:1].**

By what authority do we call this period the Great Tribulation period? By the authority of the Lord Jesus, because He used the same
language in speaking of the Great Tribulation that Daniel uses here.
He said that this would be a brief period, a time of trouble, and that
there would never be a time like it before or afterward. This is the time
the Lord Jesus called the Great Tribulation period. He knew what He
was talking about, and we will accept what He said (see Matt. 24:15–
26).

"At that time" identifies the time frame as the time of the end
(Dan. 11:35, 40; 12:4) and the latter days (Dan. 10:14). This is now
the end of the vision given to Daniel, and it ends with the Great Tribulation period. Dr. Robert Culver wrote in *Daniel and the Latter Days*,
p. 166: "Another expression, 'at the time of the end' (11:40), seems to
indicate eschatological times. I do not feel that this evidence, taken by
itself, can be pressed too far, for obviously the end of whatever series
of events is in the mind of the author is designated by the expression,
'time of the end.' This is not necessarily a series reaching on to the
consummation of the ages. However, it is quite clear from 10:14,
which fixes the scope of the prophecy to include 'the latter days,' that
the 'time of the end' in this prophecy is with reference to the period
consummated by the establishment of the Messianic kingdom."

"Michael" is identified for us here. He is the only angel given the
title of archangel (see Jude 9). His name means "who is like unto
God?" He is the one who is going to cast Satan out of heaven (see Rev.
12:7–9). He is the one who protects the nation Israel and stands in her
behalf, as Daniel makes clear here. His strategy is outlined by John in
Revelation 12:14–16.

"For the children of thy people." This is positively the nation Israel. Otherwise the language has no meaning whatsoever.

"And there shall be a time of trouble." This is the Great Tribulation
period as our Lord so labeled it in Matthew 24:21.

The believing remnant of Israel will be preserved (see Matt. 24:22; Rom. 11:26; Rev. 7:4). "And I heard the number of them which were sealed: and there were sealed an hundred and forty and four thousand of all the tribes of the children of Israel" (Rev. 7:4).

THE RESURRECTIONS OF OLD TESTAMENT SAINTS AND SINNERS

And many of them that sleep in the dust of the earth shall awake, some to everlasting life, and some to shame and everlasting contempt [Dan. 12:2].

"And many of them that sleep in the dust of the earth shall awake, some to everlasting life." The remnant of Israel living in the Great Tribulation period will be preserved, and that great company of Gentiles who are to be saved during that time also will be preserved. Those of the Old Testament who died belonging to the remnant and the Gentiles saved during the Old Testament will be raised to everlasting life at the end of the Great Tribulation.

The Old Testament saints are not raised at the Rapture of the church. Scripture clearly states that at the Rapture those ". . . which sleep in Jesus will God bring with him" (1 Thess. 4:14, italics mine). Only, ". . . the dead in Christ shall rise first" (1 Thess. 4:16, italics mine). We are in Christ by the baptism of the Holy Spirit which began on the Day of Pentecost and will end at the Rapture. This particular body of believers is called the church. We are told in 1 Corinthians 12:12-13, "For as the body is one, and hath many members, and all the members of that one body, being many, are one body: so also is Christ. For by one Spirit are we all baptized into one body, whether we be Jews or Gentiles, whether we be bond or free; and have been all made to drink into one Spirit." Christ told His disciples who were members of the nation Israel that they would be baptized by the Holy Spirit and put into the body of believers, the church—"For John truly baptized with water; but ye shall be baptized with the Holy Ghost not many days hence" (Acts 1:5).

When the church is raptured out of the world, the Old Testament

saints will not yet be raised. Why? Because the time to enter the Kingdom is at the end of the Great Tribulation period when Christ comes to
establish His Kingdom on the earth. Then the Old Testament saints
will be raised. Abraham, Isaac, and Jacob will all be raised to enter the
Kingdom on this earth at that time. However, if they were raised at the
time of the Rapture of the church, they would just have to stand
around with their harps for seven years! I think that would get a little
monotonous. However, Scripture makes it clear that they will be
raised at the end of the Great Tribulation.

"Some to shame and everlasting contempt" refers to the lost of the
Old Testament who are raised for the Great White Throne judgment at
the end of the Millennium (see Rev. 20:11–15).

**And they that be wise shall shine as the brightness of the
firmament; and they that turn many to righteousness as
the stars for ever and ever [Dan. 12:3].**

God's servants in the dark of the Great Tribulation will shine as lights.
Believers are to do the same thing today, by the way. "That ye may be
blameless and harmless, the sons of God without rebuke, in the midst
of a crooked and perverse nation, among whom ye shine as lights in
the world" (Phil. 2:15). The remnant in that day will be God's witness
in the world, and they are going to "turn many to righteousness." That
righteousness is Christ, the only righteousness which is acceptable to
God. Our righteousness is as filthy rags (see Isa. 64:6) in His sight—
not in our sight; we think we are pretty good. We pat each other on the
back and tell each other how wonderful we are, while all we produce
is a bunch of dirty laundry, my friend. God is not accepting our works;
He is accepting the righteousness of Christ, and that is provided only
by faith.

SEALING OF PROPHECY TILL
THE TIME OF THE END

**But thou, O Daniel, shut up the words, and seal the
book, even to the time of the end: many shall run to and
fro, and knowledge shall be increased [Dan. 12:4].**

These prophecies were to be sealed until "the time of the end." This does not mean the end of time but refers to that definite period of time which in the Book of Daniel is the Seventieth Week. In view of the fact that we are in the interval immediately preceding this period, it is difficult to know just how much we understand. Since so many good men differ today on the interpretation of prophecy, it would seem to indicate that there is much that we do not understand. All of this will be opened up when we reach this particular period. This is the reason we need to keep our eyes upon one thing—"Looking for that blessed hope, and the glorious appearing of the great God and our Savior Jesus Christ" (Titus 2:13).

"Many shall run to and fro." I personally believe that this refers to running up and down the Bible in study of prophecy—many shall search it through and through. There is a serious study of prophecy being made by many scholars today which has not been done in the past. Different great doctrines of the church have been studied and developed during different periods of the history of the church. At the very beginning, the doctrine of the inspiration of the Scriptures was pretty well established—also the doctrine of the deity of Christ and of redemption. Other doctrines were developed down through history. Today I think we are seeing more study of prophecy than ever before.

"Knowledge shall be increased." I believe this means knowledge of prophecy. It is true that knowledge has increased in every field today, but this refers primarily to the study of prophecy.

> **Then I Daniel looked, and, behold, there stood other two, the one on this side of the bank of the river, and the other on that side of the bank of the river.**
>
> **And one said to the man clothed in linen, which was upon the waters of the river, How long shall it be to the end of these wonders?**
>
> **And I heard the man clothed in linen, which was upon the waters of the river, when he held up his right hand and his left hand unto heaven, and sware by him that**

liveth for ever that it shall be for a time, times, and an half; and when he shall have accomplished to scatter the power of the holy people, all these things shall be finished [Dan. 12:5–7].

These verses return us to the vision which Daniel had seen at the beginning of chapter 10.

"The man clothed in linen" has been previously identified as the postincarnate Christ. Two others join Him here—one stands on one bank of the Tigris River and the other on the opposite bank. One asks how long these events will take, and the postincarnate Christ swears that it will be three and one half years, which is the last half of Daniel's Seventieth Week.

"To scatter the power of the holy people" is a strange phrase. It may mean that the rebellion of Israel will have finally been broken by the end of the Great Tribulation period and that there will have been a great turning to God at that time.

And I heard, but I understood not: then said I, O my Lord, what shall be the end of these things? [Dan. 12:8].

Though Daniel was a witness to this scene, he did not understand what he saw and heard. Daniel was puzzled and wanted to know how all of these things he had just witnessed would work out.

And he said, Go thy way, Daniel: for the words are closed up and sealed till the time of the end [Dan. 12:9].

Daniel is reminded again that these things would take place in the time of the end and are temporarily sealed (see v. 4).

THE ABOMINATION OF DESOLATION

Many shall be purified, and made white, and tried; but the wicked shall do wickedly: and none of the wicked

shall understand; but the wise shall understand [Dan. 12:10].

These great principles of God prevail from Daniel's day to the time of the end, irrespective of dispensations:

1. "Many shall be purified" refers to those who have come to Christ, "Not by works of righteousness which we have done, but according to his mercy . . ." (Titus 3:5).

2. "None of the wicked shall understand" refers to the natural man. "But the natural man receiveth not the things of the Spirit of God: for they are foolishness unto him: neither can he know them, because they are spiritually discerned" (1 Cor. 2:14).

3. "But the wise shall understand." "Howbeit when he, the Spirit of truth, is come, he will guide you into all truth: for he shall not speak of himself; but whatsoever he shall hear, that shall he speak: and he will shew you things to come" (John 16:13).

And from the time that the daily sacrifice shall be taken away, and the abomination that maketh desolate set up, there shall be a thousand two hundred and ninety days [Dan. 12:11].

The importance of this verse cannot be overemphasized as the Lord Jesus referred to it in Matthew 24:15—"When ye therefore shall see the abomination of desolation, spoken of by Daniel the prophet, stand in the holy place, (Whoso readeth, let him understand)." This is the signal to the remnant that the Great Tribulation has begun.

For 1,290 days the idol of the Beast remains in the temple. Actually, this is thirty days beyond the three and one half years. The last half of the Great Tribulation is 1,260 days, and for some unexplained reason the image of Antichrist will be permitted to remain 30 days after Antichrist himself has been cast into the lake of fire.

Blessed is he that waiteth, and cometh to the thousand three hundred and five and thirty days [Dan. 12:12].

Another series of days is given to us here with no other explanation than "blessed is he that waiteth, and cometh" to them. No one has the interpretation of this—it is sealed until the time of the end. I think sometimes we try to know more than is actually given to us.

> **But go thou thy way till the end be: for thou shalt rest, and stand in thy lot at the end of the days [Dan. 12:13].**

Daniel is told (as the Lord Jesus told Simon Peter) that he would die. He would not live to see the return of Christ, but he would be raised from the dead to enter the Millennium.

"In thy lot" means that Daniel will be raised with the Old Testament saints at the beginning of the Millennium.

"At the end of the days" brings us to the abundant entrance into Christ's kingdom. My friend, that is the future that is before us right now, a future that says Jesus is coming to this earth to establish His Kingdom. This is the hope we should keep before us in these days.

BIBLIOGRAPHY

(Recommended for Further Study)

Campbell, Donald K. *Daniel: Decoder of Dreams*. Wheaton, Illinois: Victor Books, 1977.

Criswell, W. A. *Expository Sermons on the Book of Daniel*. Grand Rapids, Michigan: Zondervan Publishing House, 1968.

DeHaan, M. R. *Daniel the Prophet*. Grand Rapids, Michigan: Zondervan Publishing House, 1947.

Gaebelein, Arno C. *The Prophet Daniel*. Neptune, New Jersey: Loizeaux Brothers, 1911.

Ironside, H. A. *Lectures on Daniel the Prophet*. Neptune, New Jersey: Loizeaux Brothers, 1911. (Especially good for young Christians.)

Kelly, William. *Lectures on the Book of Daniel*. Addison, Illinois: Bible Truth Publishers, 1881.

Larkin, Clarence. *The Book of Daniel*. Philadelphia: The Larkin Estate, 1929. (Very helpful charts.)

Luck, G. Coleman. *Daniel*. Chicago, Illinois: Moody Press, 1958. (Fine, inexpensive survey.)

McClain, Alva J. *Daniel's Prophecy of the Seventy Weeks*. Winona Lake, Indiana: Brethren Missionary Herald Co., 1940.

McGee, J. Vernon. *Delving Through Daniel*. Pasadena, California: Thru the Bible Books, 1960.

Strauss, Lehman. *The Prophecies of Daniel*. Neptune, New Jersey: Loizeaux Brothers, 1969. (Very practical.)

Walvoord, John F. *Daniel, The Key to Prophetic Revelation*. Chicago, Illinois: Moody Press, 1971. (Excellent, comprehensive interpretation.)

Wood, Leon J. *Daniel: A Study Guide Commentary*. Grand Rapids, Michigan: Zondervan Publishing House, 1975. (Excellent for individual and group study.)

HELPFUL BOOKS ON BIBLE PROPHECY

Hoyt, Hermann A. *The End Times*. Chicago, Illinois: Moody Press, 1969.

Pentecost, J. Dwight. *Things to Come*. Grand Rapids, Michigan: Zondervan Publishing House, 1958.

Ryrie, Charles C. *The Basis of the Premillennial Faith*. Neptune, New Jersey: Loizeaux Brothers, 1953.

Ryrie, Charles C. *What You Should Know About the Rapture*. Chicago, Illinois: Moody Press, 1981.

Sauer, Erich. *From Eternity to Eternity*. Grand Rapids, Michigan: Wm. B. Eerdmans Publishing Co., 1954.

Tatford, Frederick A. *The Minor Prophets*. Minneapolis, Minnesota: Klock & Klock, n.d.

Walvoord, John F. *Armageddon, Oil, and the Middle East Crisis*. Grand Rapids, Michigan: Zondervan Publishing House, 1974.

Walvoord, John F. *The Millennial Kingdom*. Grand Rapids, Michigan: Zondervan Publishing House, 1959.

Walvoord, John F. *The Rapture Question*. Grand Rapids, Michigan: Zondervan Publishing House, 1957.

Wood, Leon J. *The Bible and Future Events*. Grand Rapids, Michigan: Zondervan Publishing House, 1973.